MORE THAN MARMALADE

Michael Bond and the Story of Paddington Bear

Rosanne Tolin

CHICAGO
REVIEW
PRESS

Copyright © 2020 by Rosanne Tolin
All rights reserved
Published by Chicago Review Press Incorporated
814 North Franklin Street
Chicago, Illinois 60610
ISBN 978-1-64160-314-0

Library of Congress Control Number:2019955532

Interior design: Sarah Olson
Map design: Chris Erichsen

Printed in the United States of America
5 4 3 2 1

For Hal, Josie, Jack, Danny, and AJ,
life would be un*bear*able without you all in it.

To my Dad,
the only person I know who read
War and Peace just for fun.

Contents

Author's Note

I clearly recall my first introduction to Paddington Bear. I was eight years old, and my second-grade teacher lent me her only copy of author Michael Bond's delightful *A Bear Called Paddington* during silent reading time. Immediately, I adored the small, bumbling bear who tried mightily to fit in with his new family far from home.

It's no wonder Bond's Paddington Bear books have captivated readers for half a century. Never wallowing in his rather unfortunate circumstances, Paddington has charmed children and adults alike with his amusing mishaps. Even though his first book was published in 1958, Bond's endearing tales deal with issues we still think about today. Like many immigrants looking for a

Michael Bond and Paddington Bear pose for a picture at the Menzies Hotel. *Nigel Peter Todd/Fairfax Media via Getty Images*

better life, Paddington Bear was seeking a fresh start in a foreign land. He arrived in London alone, knowing no one, but hoping to begin anew. The refugees fleeing to safer places were part of Paddington's story, too. Even more than his favorite marmalade sandwich!

Many of the details in the Paddington book series are based on real events. The fictional bear's story emerges from war trauma and remains as relevant today as it was when Bond created him in the 1950s. Bond, who died at 91 in 2017, was a young teenager in London when World War II broke out. Before the fighting began, and for months afterward, he watched German Jewish children struggle to escape the Nazis. Thousands arrived in England, leaving their parents behind. The British people promised to look after them. These children, uprooted from their homeland, often had nothing but a knapsack full of clothes.

Like many of them, Paddington Bear was an orphan. He'd lost both his parents in an earthquake. With no family to help, Paddington hid on a ship bound for England. Arriving in London with only a small suitcase (and everything he owned tucked inside), the stowaway cub stood alone on Platform 1 in Paddington Station. There he waited patiently for a family to adopt him. A tag around his neck read PLEASE LOOK AFTER THIS BEAR. THANK YOU. The tag was a real-life detail Bond remembered from the war. Refugee children and evacuees sent to Britain wore tags displaying their names and ages.

Though he was just 13 when war broke out, Bond had seen news reels about terrible things the Nazis were doing to their own citizens. He knew these things were wrong. When he wrote *A Bear Called Paddington* 19 years later, he gave Paddington a warm shelter with a loving family—something he wished for those frightened German Jewish children.

Throughout his life, Bond sympathized with refugees. His stories reflect the confusion of coming to an unfamiliar place. Immigrants need to learn new languages. They have to figure out customs that differ from their own. In a letter (from Paddington) written a decade ago, Bond protested the United Kingdom Border Detention Center's unjust treatment of young refugees:

> Whenever I hear about children from foreign countries being put into detention centres, I think how lucky I am to be living at number 32 Windsor Gardens with such nice people as Mr. and Mrs. Brown. Mrs. Bird, who looks after the Browns, says if she had her way she would set the children free, and lock up a few politicians in their place to see how they liked it!

Fortunately for Paddington, the Brown family adopted the bear "from darkest Peru" and helped him adapt. Of course, Paddington's life still wasn't easy. He tried hard to do the right thing, but often, he ended up making a mess. The trouble he caused always needed to be untangled, which is much of what made Paddington's escapades so much fun.

Altogether, Bond wrote over 150 chapter-length stories for the books. Fifteen Paddington novels have been translated into 40 languages and have sold more than 35 million copies. By writing about Paddington's adventures, Bond gave all those lost and lonely children from World War II a happy ending.

Today, Paddington is as adored as ever, thanks to the recent success of big-screen movies based on the series. The debut film, released in 2014 and simply titled *Paddington*, delighted Michael Bond himself.

Like his hopeful bear, the author's remarkable story begs to be told in this time of domestic and international unrest. Though details of Bond's childhood are limited, it was possible to piece them together using his own words. While some of the author's quotes in this book have been adapted to better fit a middle grade biography, they have been taken from verifiable sources. This book is a rare account of his life, with fictionalized scenes based in fact to paint an intimate picture of a modest man. Bond really did carry on lengthy conversations with Paddington Bear! In fact, Paddington was so much a personal friend and part of the family that, to this day, the original bear—rescued from a store shelf on Christmas Eve—has never appeared in public.

I sincerely hope you enjoy reading *More than Marma-lade*, a biography of a pair of the world's most inspiring characters, as much as I enjoyed writing it!

Bear-y Truly Yours,
Rosanne Tolin

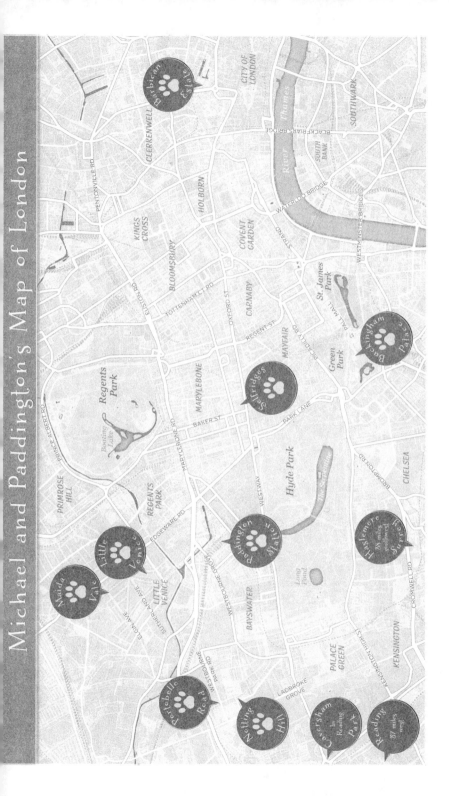

Trains, Books, and Bears

**"Things are always happening to me.
I'm that sort of bear."**

–MICHAEL BOND IN *A BEAR CALLED PADDINGTON*

Thomas Michael Bond pushed his way through the crowd of people standing on the railway platform. He was 10 years old, and although he stood on his toes, the tall adults waiting to board the Cornish Riviera Express train blocked his view. He *needed* to get closer before it disappeared down the tracks.

The steam powered engine charged toward the platform, spouting clouds of thick smoke into the sky. Its engine, fueled by burning coal, tugged at least 13 passenger cars. They rattled into the station, hissing like a snake.

"Pardon me, sir!" Michael called. "Pardon me, ma'am!"

At last he popped out at the front edge of the crowd. Just then, the train puffed and wheezed to a stop. What a sight! It was 1936 and the locomotive was one of the largest trains operating on the Great Western Railway. Mesmerized by its enormous size, Michael barely noticed all the people clamoring to climb aboard.

Once the passengers disappeared inside the steel carriages, only Michael was left on the platform. With a sputter and a low chuffing sound, the train started back down the track. Bursts of white steam sprayed from the chimney stack. The piercing whistle made Michael cover his large ears, which looked like they'd been molded from clay.

Although the noise was painful to hear, every sound the train made enchanted him. The rods that drove the wheels clunked back and forth. The cars rattled and clanked. A narrow funnel poured fine gravel on the tracks to help the wheels grip the rails. If Michael listened closely, he could hear the heavy locomotive crunching the sand.

"Are you lost, lad?" A man in a blue conductor's uniform startled him.

"No sir," said Michael, snapping out of his gaze. In his daydream, he had seen his own name painted on the front of the train. How long had he been standing there?

Locomotives continued to captivate Michael his entire life. He would frequently walk to nearby Reading Station just to get a glimpse of the massive Express roaring by.

● ● ● ● ●

Born in 1926 in Berkshire, England, Michael moved with his family to the bigger city of Reading when he was still a baby. They lived on one side of a duplex home with a large yard all around the house. The name of Michael's town was appropriate since inside his boyhood home, the rooms were packed with books.

"I was fortunate," Michael said, "to be brought up in a house where books were part of the furniture."

Both of his parents supported Michael's love of reading. His father, a postal worker, gave him a subscription to a comic book that came out weekly called *Magnet*. Michael devoured page after page of its detective stories and tales of adventure.

Michael's mother read even more than he did. Every week, she went to the public library to check out new books. Michael always tagged along. The wide aisles filled with thick hardbacks thrilled him. He slowly wandered through the stacks to see what might catch his eye.

At the time, several well-known stories featured bears. *Winnie-the-Pooh* had arrived in Britain the year Michael was born and was still popular. Another favorite still in publication today was *Rupert Bear*, a comic strip character in the *Daily Express* newspaper.

Once Michael picked out an armful of library books, he met his mother at the checkout counter. He neatly stacked his pile next to the ones she had carefully collected.

"My!" said the librarian. "What a great many books you have chosen, young man! You must love to read."

"Yes, miss," Michael said politely.

The librarian beamed. "I see you've been taught proper manners."

"Thank you, madam."

He bundled his books with a stiff leather strap to make them easier to carry. Then he and his mother set off for home. Sometimes they strolled through a park called Forbury Gardens. When they took that route, they passed the Maiwand Lion statue, a war memorial built in 1884.

Michael stared in amazement at the imposing bronze structure. Reminders of many battles England fought were all around him. World War I had ended less than 10 years before he was born, and the Royal Berkshire

Maiwand Lion statue in Forbury Gardens, Reading, England.
Amanda Lewis/Dreamstime

Regiment War Memorial honored those soldiers. Grown-ups still remembered that awful time. Thousands of young lives were lost, leaving grieving families behind. Michael often heard stories of the "lean years" when things like milk, meat, and butter were in short supply. Back then, even King George and Queen Mary used ration cards issued by the British government.

As Michael and his mother walked through town, they waved hello to people they recognized. Now and then the two of them stopped to chat with friends. Since there was no reason to hurry, they picked up jam tarts at the local bakery. Michael's mother allowed him to savor one as they sauntered along. He let the sweet raspberry filling linger on his tongue.

Back at home, Michael set his books on the kitchen table. His stack made a satisfying *whump* as it landed on the checkered cloth. He had a lot of reading to do! As usual, he tried his best to keep up with his mom. Michael always told people that "she practically read a book a day."

Michael's mother loved reading so much that she took time to thank the authors. Later that day, she tapped Michael on the shoulder.

"Shall we write a letter?" she asked.

"Who shall we write to today, Mummy?"

"Another novelist!" said his mother.

She retrieved a book she had checked out of the library. The detective story was her favorite from the week before. Determined to find more clues, she had decided to borrow it a second time.

"Fetch the good paper from your father's desk," she said.

Michael sprinted down the hall and pulled a few sheets of crisp, white writing paper from the desk drawer. He knew it was expensive, so he was careful not to crease the edges. When he got back to the kitchen, his mother was already seated at the table.

The book was open to a passage she had practically memorized. While her index finger followed in a straight line, Michael skimmed the words. They fit together perfectly, like the last few pieces of a jigsaw puzzle.

Then Michael and his mother wrote a letter that went something like this:

Dear Sir,

I have had the distinct pleasure of reading your latest book. The people you write about come alive on the page. Many delightful hours passed when I read the story the first time. I plan to read it again!

Yours sincerely,

Mrs. Frances M. Bond

Michael admired his mother's perfect penmanship. She used a dip pen, so he gave the ink a minute to dry. Then he carefully folded the letter while his mom wrote the publisher's address on an envelope. Once she sealed it, he took it back down the hallway, past the staircase, and stepped outside. He placed the letter in the small metal box hanging beside the front door. By the time he returned inside, his mother was cooking dinner.

"Why don't you take Binkie into the garden and have a bit of fun?" his mother suggested. She wiped her hands on her apron. Oily smudges dotted its cotton smock like splattered paint.

"Come on, Binkie!" Michael said.

He clapped his hands and the family dog came running. Binkie looked a lot like a terrier and was mostly white with black spots on both ears. They hurried into the backyard where there was space to throw a ball.

Binkie loved to run after the ball and bring it back to Michael. Sometimes Binkie would pretend to bring it back only to veer away at the last second. Michael ended up chasing him and laughing the entire time.

When they were both out of breath, they went back inside. Binkie flopped down on the cool kitchen floor. Michael grabbed his books off the table and headed up to his room. The second he walked in, a chorus of squeals greeted him.

"Hi, Pip!" he called as he closed the door behind him. "Hello, Squeak!"

He approached a cage that held three plump guinea pigs.

"Hi, Wilfred!" he greeted the third ball of fur.

Michael turned around to balance the stack of books on his bed. Then carefully, he scooped each guinea pig up out of the cage. He lowered them to the floor where they immediately ran off to investigate his room. One went under the dresser while the other shot over to the wall. The third followed Michael to his bed. When the boy flopped down on his mattress, Wilfred sat up on his hind legs and sniffed the air.

Michael loved to let his pet guinea pigs run free. His mother didn't like that much, but she said it was all right as long as they stayed in his room. He picked up a book of animal fables and began reading aloud. Squeak especially was soothed by the sound of Michael's voice. She crawled under the bed and closed her eyes.

After reading for an hour, Michael fell asleep with his head on the open book. His mother called up the stairs, waking him from his nap.

"Come eat your supper, Michael!"

Michael swooped up Wilfred and Pip right away. He reached for Squeak, but she slipped out of his palm and burrowed farther beneath the bed. After a quick game of chase, Michael caught her and gently lowered her into the cage.

"Sorry," Michael apologized as he closed the barred door. "I'll let you out again later!"

He raced down the steps and into the kitchen. His father was home and took his seat at the table. His mom had made "bubble and squeak"—patties formed from bacon and roasted vegetables, fried, and topped with an egg—for dinner. The dish was called bubble and squeak because of the funny sounds the patties made as they cooked.

After eating their fill, the family discussed all the things they had done that day. When it was Michael's father's turn to talk, tales of the mail room took over. Once the dishes were cleared and Binkie was fed, Michael's mother rotated the radio dial to Duke Ellington's Orchestra. She sat down with a book, the sound of jazz music spreading throughout the room like a smooth, snug blanket. Next came the time that Michael liked most.

"What story would you like to hear?" his father asked.

"A new one!" Michael said. "I picked it out already."

Since Michael was too old for picture books, his father read children's novels to him every night. It was a special way for them to spend time together. They went upstairs, and Michael pointed to a book he had set on his nightstand. He dove under the covers while his father sat on the edge of the bed.

Opening to the first page, his father began to read. The next day, Michael finished the next five chapters when he got home from school. At bedtime, his father would read to him from the point where Michael had stopped.

Every night, his father's voice relaxed him. His home was safe and calm. The smell of his mother's lavender bath salts drifted down the hall into his bedroom. In the corner, Pip, Squeak, and Wilfred rustled around in their cage. Soon they settled in and went to sleep. Michael drifted off, dreaming about the story his father had read to him from the library book.

Mishaps and Mischief

Michael always had a big imagination. He found amusement in things that others might find boring. He carried this lighthearted way of looking at life into adulthood.

Taking himself too seriously was something Michael naturally avoided. He loved to play practical jokes, like adding salt to the sugar bowl. When his father put a spoonful in his tea, he was surprised at the terrible taste! Playing tricks wasn't the only way Michael used comedy. By finding the silly side of mistakes, he made others feel better about their faults.

Michael's teachers did not always share his view of things. They wanted their students to be quiet and studious. Once, a report sent home for his parents had a handwritten note attached. The note read, "Bond suffers from a distorted sense of humor." Although it was meant to be stern, Michael thought that was very funny.

In school, he only managed to make average grades. He didn't mind that much because he came home to a family he adored and a houseful of books. His father was known to be clumsy but was always ready to laugh at his fumbles. Every mishap his dad made became another story for Michael to tell his friends.

One summer day, he and his father went outside to play. The sun was shining, and the backyard stretched a long way down to the fence. Binkie flopped down in a patch of shade. It was too hot to play fetch. The park in Reading would be cooler with the breeze blowing through. It was the perfect day to go for a bike ride.

Michael loved to ride his bike all around town. His dad also cycled to work. If they rode their bicycles, they would be at the park in no time. And the wind would fan them on the ride over.

"Let's ride the push bikes to the park," Michael said. "Maybe I can find enough boys to play cricket."

"First, I have an idea," his father said, puffing out his chest. "I challenge you to a race."

"You're on!" Michael said.

"The starting line is here at the back door."

"And the finish line is the fence!"

They mounted their bicycles. Long and lanky, Michael was outgrowing his, and only his toes fit firmly on the pedals. Back then, no one wore helmets or knee-pads when they rode. They didn't worry about falling. The grass in the yard was thick and soft. If anything happened, Michael and his father would land safely on a green cushion.

"Take your mark!" his dad said.

They inched their bikes backward until the rear tires touched the side of the house. Then they each planted one foot firmly on a pedal. Michael looked up. His dad's eyes sparkled mischievously. He was an adult, but he always played hard just like a kid!

"Ready?" Michael asked.

"Steady!" his dad said.

"Go!" Michael shouted.

They both took off. Even though his dad grabbed the lead, Michael quickly accelerated. He pumped those pedals for all he was worth and soared past his father. They were only halfway down the yard when Michael pulled ahead. He could not see his dad anymore.

He kept gaining speed until the fence loomed in front of him. Then he smashed down hard on the brakes. Throwing himself to one side, he skidded to a stop. Just as the rear tire whapped into the fence, his right foot touched down on the grass. He was first—he had won!

But where was his father? He should have been at the fence already. Michael turned around expecting to see his dad flying toward him. Instead, the yard was empty.

"Papa?" he called.

He heard a low muttering and a gasping laugh from behind the shed. When Michael ran back and peeked around the side, he saw his father lying flat on the ground. His bike had keeled over onto the grass. One wheel spun crazily. A black smudge marked where the bicycle tire had smacked into the shed.

"Papa, are you all right?" Michael asked.

"Well, strike me pink," his dad said, shaking his head. He sat up and brushed grass off his sleeve.

"You are so fast," his dad said. "I had to do something drastic to catch up. It most definitely did not work out the way I planned."

"What did you do?" Michael asked.

"I tried to reduce drag. So I made myself smaller by putting my head down."

"But," Michael began, looking confused, "then you couldn't see where you were going."

"It would have been worth it if I had won." They both clutched their stomachs from laughing so hard.

Many stories like this one would remain in Michael's memory. He was lucky his father liked to have fun.

Occasionally his dad's habits seemed odd to other people. His father was a courteous gentleman even when it wasn't expected. In fact, he was so well mannered, he sometimes did strange things.

One story Michael recalled took place on their family vacation. Whenever they took a trip, they went to a beach on the Isle of Wight. Every time, his dad would roll up his trousers and wade into the water. Even while out in the ocean, he still wanted to be able to tip his cap.

"He used to go in the sea," Michael said, "and keep his hat on in case he met someone he knew."

Now, that's a respectful man!

For Michael and his father, doing everyday chores together could be entertaining. Brushing Binkie's coat became a competition for the biggest fur ball. Making beards from a mountain of suds made washing dishes less of a bother. Lucky for Michael, role models in his life made the dull moments more exciting.

● ● ● ● ●

Because so many soldiers had lost their lives in World War I, Michael's neighborhood had far more women than men. Many of the women who had lost their husbands or adult sons offered to babysit him.

"It was a mixed blessing," Michael said later. "The women were lonely for a very sad reason."

He was frequently invited over to their homes for a meal or part of a weekend. To make it easier to remember their names, he often called these women "Auntie So-and-So." They weren't really related to him, but they loved him as if he were their nephew.

Auntie Emm helped tidy the house and got Michael off to school when his parents were busy. Two other "aunts" were Auntie Annie and Auntie Gee. They owned a dog kennel near Greenham Common, a Royal Air Force station. Michael loved to visit them because he could also see their dogs. Planes roared overhead while he took them for walks. The best part was when the two women took him to the movies.

"Would you like to go to the cinema?" Auntie Gee asked.

Auntie Gee was nearly deaf, but she did not need to hear in order to understand what people said. She had taught herself how to read lips. Whenever Michael talked to her, she peered closely at his mouth.

"Yes, I would like to see the picture show, please," Michael said.

"Such a polite lad," she said approvingly.

Their outings included a stop at the snack bar. Popcorn had not always been sold inside theaters. Snack bars were fairly new. When cinemas first started showing films, they were as fancy as theaters that staged live plays. The last thing movie theater managers wanted was popcorn and candy ruining their elegant carpets.

As time went by, things changed. The street vendors that once sold popcorn outside the cinemas moved inside. Eventually the movie theaters began selling treats, too. By the time Michael went to the picture show with his aunts, the snack bar had become a regular part of their outing. Eating popcorn and candy bars was as much a part of their trip as sitting in the plush, velvet seats.

The first time Michael accompanied these two women to the theater, he worried about Auntie Gee. If she couldn't hear him talking to her up close, how could she ever hear the actors on the screen? Maybe her lip-reading trick would work for watching a film, too.

It turned out that she could only lip-read if she sat next to the person who was talking. She couldn't read the lips of the actors on the screen. Auntie Annie wasn't about to let Auntie Gee miss out on the latest love story or comedy, however. She had an idea of her own: every time they headed out to see a film, Auntie Annie slipped a flashlight into her purse. The first time Michael saw her do that, he misunderstood.

"Are you worried about tripping in the dark?" he asked. "I can hold your hand so you won't fall."

"What a sweet boy!" Auntie Annie said. "No, the flashlight is for something else. Just you wait and see."

The movie theater wasn't far away, so they walked over. Michael couldn't stop thinking about the mysterious flashlight tucked in her purse. What in the world would she use it for? The beam would disturb people trying to watch the film. He worried that she would be yelled at. Even worse, he thought the usher might throw Auntie Annie out.

He shouldn't have worried one bit. They stopped at the snack bar, where each of them picked out their favorite candy and a bucket of popcorn. Then they made their way into the theater and found three empty seats. As the lights dimmed, a heavy scarlet curtain rose to reveal the enormous movie screen.

The first thing the audience saw was a set of news reels. Televisions were still expensive, and few people owned them. Most still relied on radio broadcasts for information. Going to the movies was the only way they could view updates about important current events. Every theater showed the movie only after running the latest news reels.

The moment the first reel began, Auntie Annie took the flashlight out of her purse. She switched on the light and aimed it at her mouth. She'd carefully selected an aisle seat so she could lean forward without distracting anyone. Auntie Annie whispered every word the reporter said, while Auntie Gee read her lips.

As soon as the news reels ended, the movie started. The flashlight stayed on the entire time, and Auntie Annie repeated every word the actors spoke. Auntie Gee might have been hard of hearing, but a little ingenuity allowed her to enjoy the movie as much as anyone else.

With the company of kind, clever ladies like Auntie Gee and Auntie Annie, young Michael stayed occupied while his parents worked or did household chores. But the activities they had planned for him weren't always as enjoyable as going to the cinema. Since she helped in the evenings too, Auntie Emm insisted Michael needed a bath before bed. Even if he didn't agree!

As if washing up weren't already bad enough for a boy, Auntie Emm chain-smoked cigarettes. Back then, people didn't know they were harmful. Michael didn't like cigarettes at all. Just the smell made him cough. Still, Auntie Emm puffed on one right after the other, even while she was giving him a bath.

"The ash used to fall all over me," Michael said.

So much for getting clean!

●　●　●　●　●

One morning, Michael went to school like any other day. He really enjoyed being with his friends, but he didn't particularly like class. Sometimes he pretended to be sick so his mother would let him stay home. His distaste for school had started with naptime when he was eight years old.

"Children used to have a half an hour sleep after lunch," Michael recalled years later. "I can still picture the dreadful blankets and their smell." The blankets were probably wool. When the air was damp, they let off an unpleasant stench. Imagine being forced to nap underneath a scratchy, stinky blanket!

Things were always better when school let out for the day. Soon after Michael's father got home from work, they usually played board games like checkers. When Michael was older, he often said, "My father's motto was, 'The most precious gift you can bestow on a child is your time.'"

On this particular day, however, his father had been clumsier than usual. He had ended up seeing a doctor at the hospital. Michael ran into his parents' bedroom and found his father bundled up in bed. A sling held his arm close to his body.

"What happened, Papa?" Michael asked.

"Oh, nothing much," his dad said matter-of-factly.

"Your father broke his collarbone," his mother said. "He fell off his bike."

Michael couldn't help but tease his dad about the bicycle race that had gone wrong in their backyard.

"Did you run into the shed again?" he asked with a smile.

"Not quite," his father said, wincing as he held back a laugh. "I was riding along the street when my wheels dropped down into the tram tracks."

Ouch! Michael had gotten his bicycle tires caught in the tram tracks before. Once a wheel dropped into the rut, it was impossible to steer anywhere except along the track. He always had to stop and lift the bike out of the rut. Half the time, the bike wobbled so much that he tipped over before he could stop.

"You fell when the wheel went into the track?" Michael asked.

"Not at all!" his father said. "The tram line goes right past the post office building, so I didn't need to stop. I just allowed the bike to roll along in the tram track."

"Wow! That was really clever of you," Michael said.

"It was," his father agreed. "Until I got to work. That's when I fell."

"After all those miles?" Michael asked. "Your whole ride was fine, but you fell once you got there?"

Even though it made his dad's broken bone hurt a little more, they both started giggling.

Just then Michael's grandfather arrived. He wanted to make sure everyone was all right after the accident. Once he heard the story, he laughed right along with the rest of them.

When it was time for his grandfather to go, Michael walked him to the door. The two of them were especially close. Suddenly, his grandpa grew serious. He put one hand on his grandson's shoulder and looked him straight in the eyes.

"You know I think very highly of you, Michael," he said. "Remember you can do anything you want with your life, anything at all."

"I want to join the Royal Air Force," Michael said. "I see the planes take off whenever I visit Auntie Annie and Auntie Gee. They roar up into the clouds!"

His grandfather nodded. "You can do anything with your life," he said, "but you must stick with it. Never give up. Keep going, and one day you'll find yourself doing exactly what you want."

Those words would come back to Michael later in life. He spent many years writing articles and short stories. Only after a long struggle would his work finally be published. Through all that time, he would stick with it. He would never stop trying to share his work with the world.

The World at War

I n 1939, when Michael was 13 years old, news reels he saw at the movies frightened him. The Nazi party had recently risen to power in Germany. They took advantage of the country's weakness during the world-wide Great Depression to grow in political strength. Members claimed Jewish people were the reason for the nation's troubles. Blaming them was an easy excuse for the country's mounting poverty.

Nazis were led by a man named Adolf Hitler. Feeding into anger felt by many citizens after Germany's loss in World War I, he promised to return the nation to its "rightful position" as a world leader. Fear of a Communist takeover made the German people feel even more helpless. By 1933 Hitler had turned his role as the head of Germany's government into a Nazi dictatorship.

For many years, anti-Jewish boycotts were staged. Stormtroopers—*Stoßtruppen*—stood in front of Jewish-owned stores and offices to block the entrances. The Star of David was drawn in yellow and black paint on their buildings. Nazis claimed Jewish businesspeople threatened to take over everything. Signs printed by the government claimed, "The Jews Are Our Misfortune."

Whenever everyday citizens violently attacked Jewish people, the police looked the other way. Jewish workers were fired from their jobs at universities, hospitals, and schools. Book burnings helped build Hitler's power by destroying anything that didn't match his extreme ideas. Rules like the 1935 Nuremberg Laws proclaimed people of Nordic descent, called the "Aryan race," were above everyone else. Hitler heralded Aryans as the only pure German population. All others, especially Jews, Romani, and those of African lineage, were considered inferior.

Michael watched bits and pieces of Hitler's actions on the movie screen. News reels showed mobs destroying Jewish homes and buildings. He also saw footage of Nazi soldiers forcing Jewish people into ghettos, areas that would be walled off from the rest of society. The Jewish people were only allowed to take what they could carry. Many hauled their life's possessions like loads of wood, piling their belongings into baby strollers—prams—or wheelbarrows.

The images stayed with Michael all his life. Later, he described the "footage of elderly people pushing prams with all their belongings in them." He always shook his head with disbelief at the thought of these grim scenes.

After the movie was over, Michael walked home. His family still lived in Reading, which was close to London. The streets around the train station were packed with

Young World War II refugees arrive at England's train stations wearing tags of identification. *PA Images/Alamy Stock Photo*

people who had come from the city. Every one of them carried small suitcases, bags, and other packages filled with their possessions. They looked just like the refugees he had seen in the news reels.

Michael was shocked when he realized that most of them were children. They flooded off the trains and wandered around the platforms. Only a few of them were with their parents. Some of the children were so scared that they were crying. Others ran outside the station to the sidewalk and looked all around. They were curious about the strange new place where they would be living.

Most of the kids wore a large tag hanging from a piece of string like a necklace. *What is that for?*, Michael wondered. When Michael passed one boy, he stopped to look at the cardboard box he carried. Many of the children held similar containers.

"What's in there?" Michael asked.

"A gas mask," the boy said.

"Blimey! Is it a real one?"

"It's real, all right," the boy said. "It'll save me if we're attacked with poisonous gas."

He opened the box so that Michael could peer inside. The smell of the mask's rubber was strong. Two glass lenses stared up at him like blank eyes.

"Why are you wearing that tag?" Michael asked.

"It's got my name and my age on this side." The boy flipped the card over to the back side. "Those are the names of me mum and dad. And that's my home address."

"In case you get lost?" Michael asked.

"Sort of. The tag will make sure my name is recorded in the files here in Reading," he answered. "That way, my parents will know where I am."

"When will you go back home?" Michael asked.

The boy shrugged. "No one really knows. They said I might not even have to go to school while I'm here."

Michael felt a stab of jealousy. "Why not? I have to go to school."

"There isn't enough room for all of us."

The crowd of children overwhelmed the town. Reading's school buildings could never fit them all inside. Some teachers would work double shifts to teach one group in the morning and another group in the afternoon. Still, many of the kids would not attend school for months.

Michael had learned about the evacuation of London through the news reels. The evacuation was called Operation Pied Piper. The Nazis were marching closer and closer to starting a new war. Operation Pied Piper was intended to save as many British children and their mothers as possible.

Nations around the world were scared of what the Nazis might do. Because England had suffered so much during World War I, everyone knew terrible things might happen if another war broke out. During World War I, the German army had bombed the United Kingdom more than 50 times. The first bombs had been dropped from blimps, giant airships called dirigibles. Later, fighter airplanes dropped bombs.

No matter how the bombs were delivered, many British civilians were killed. It had taken years to recover from all the death and destruction. The government wasn't about to let that happen again. As Hitler's actions grew more violent, the United Kingdom began moving people out of large cities such as London. Those were the places most likely to be bombed again.

Even though many mothers evacuated with their children, not everyone was able to leave the cities together. There just weren't enough shelters to house them in the countryside. Pregnant women were sent to smaller towns before women who were not. Teenagers and very young children traveled without their parents. As they got off the trains and buses, police officers and adult volunteers rushed over to help.

"Here we are," said one policeman. "This nice lady will take you to your new home."

"I want my mummy!" cried a small boy.

"There, there," said the volunteer. She took the boy's hand. "We are going to find you a nice place to stay for a little while. A place where you will be cared for."

Michael followed the throng of children over to the town hall. A government official lined them up against a long wall. The line was so long that it curved around the building.

"I'll take that one," a man said as he pointed to a girl.

"It's me and me sister." The girl grabbed the hand of a younger girl at her side. "We don't go nowhere without the other."

"All right, then," the man said. "I'll take you both."

The government officer in Reading recorded the names of both girls on a piece of paper. He wrote down the name and address of the man who would take them home and care for them. All up and down the line, adults and couples were pointing to other kids. They would take home as many as they could. As long as the cities remained dangerous, the houses and apartments in Reading and other small towns would be the children's temporary homes.

Michael tugged at the shirt of the man who was writing down names and addresses.

"Excuse me, sir," he said. "What will happen to the children who aren't taken?"

"They will go to orphanages and farms," the man said. "Don't worry lad. Every one of them will be safe." Michael didn't feel so sure.

The first evacuation lasted four days. Thousands of people moved out of London into the countryside. As the war unfolded, additional evacuations sent more people away from big cities. More than 3.5 million civilians were relocated.

"It made a great impression on me," Michael said, "seeing those lost and frightened people."

As he walked home that day, he had forgotten all about the movie. His mind was crammed full of thoughts about the children dropped into a new place with only strangers to take care of them. After seeing the children arrive in Reading, Michael had never felt so fortunate to have a secure, carefree home.

● ● ● ● ●

Later that year, the changes taking place in the world changed his family's life, too. His father joined the Home Guard—a citizen's militia providing support to the British military. This armed force included men over 40 years old who wanted to serve their country but otherwise couldn't. To further help the war effort, Michael's parents volunteered to care for two refugee boys. One of the boys was around 9 years old, and the other was around 10. After getting the boys settled, Michael's mom and dad came into his room.

"We want you to know that we won't let anything happen to you," his father said quietly, stroking Michael's hair. Rarely had he seen his dad this serious. Michael swallowed the lump that swelled in his throat.

"Are children still coming from London?" he asked.

"No," said his mother. "Now they are arriving all the way from Germany."

"Are the German people afraid that their towns will be bombed, too?" Michael asked.

"I'm afraid it's much worse than that," she said.

"The children are in danger because of who they are," his father said.

"Do you remember the news reels you saw a few months ago?" his mother asked. "About Kristallnacht?"

"The Night of Broken Glass," Michael whispered in a hushed voice.

His father nodded. "The Nazis have spread their hatred for Jews beyond Germany. It has spread to parts of Austria, and the areas in Czechoslovakia that German soldiers have overrun."

"For two nights," his mother said, "innocent Jewish people were terrorized. Their homes and businesses were destroyed. Broken glass covered the streets."

"Our prime minister is an upstanding man," his father said. "Mr. Chamberlain is allowing Jewish and Quaker leaders here in England to bring children to our country. Any child up to the age of 17 can come."

"The ones who are in danger of being arrested," his mother said, "are the first to arrive."

"Why would the Nazis arrest kids?" Michael asked.

"Because they are Jewish," she said. "Or because they are being blamed for helping Communists."

"The rest," his father said, "are Polish children being threatened with deportation. Or they are Jewish orphans, or they are children whose families are poor."

"The really unlucky children have parents in the concentration camps," his mother said. These "camps" were prisons where millions of innocent Jews would die under Hitler's command.

"The two boys we took in, will they be safe here?" Michael asked.

"Most definitely," his father said. "We won't let anyone hurt them."

"What about all the other children?" Michael asked. "So many already came from London. Is there any space left for more?"

"The government is helping," said his mother. "Any family who takes in a child immigrant from the Kindertransport is guaranteed to receive 50 British pounds."

The Kindertransport referred to efforts made by Great Britain to rescue as many refugee Jewish children as possible. Fifty pounds in 1939 would be worth nearly $4,500 in 2020.

"Our government expects that 5,000 kids will come." His father shook his head. "But there is no limit to the number who are welcome here. Our country will take as many as need safety."

By the time the war began, around 10,000 children had fled to England. Over 1,000 more were taken in by the United States. Canada, Australia, South Africa, and New Zealand each took in hundreds of refugees. Another 14,000 children were sent by their families to other countries to live with relatives.

The last Kindertransport group left Germany on September 1, 1939, right as World War II began. Often, these children were the only members of their families to survive the Holocaust. They began their new lives with only the few things that could fit into a single small suitcase. The journey saw the children travel by train across Germany and through Holland. From there they traveled by boat across the English Channel to England.

They were allowed to carry only 10 German marks, worth about $70 today. Most couldn't speak English and had no idea who would be caring for them. With the help of British citizens, they started new lives.

Some of the Kindertransport children grew up and did great things. Adre Asriel would compose music for film sound tracks. Frank Auerbach became a famous British painter. Leslie Brent worked as a scientist with the National Institute for Medical Research. Rolf Decker became a professional soccer player who competed with the US Olympic team. German American sculptor Eva Hesse's life was made into a film in 2016. Lily Renee Wilhelm illustrated comic books like *The Werewolf Hunter* and *The Lost World*.

Because England and other countries saved them, these people made the world better through science, art, and sport. The impact of the Kindertransport and the British evacuations didn't stop there. Years later, the events would inspire children's writers. Authors started to think about how it would feel for a young child to go somewhere without his or her parents. Scary, definitely. Exciting too, because without a mother or father around to lay down the rules, the kids could do things their own way.

C. S. Lewis wrote a book series about kids in a similar situation. In the first book, *The Lion, the Witch and the Wardrobe*, children are evacuated from London to a large manor house in the country. When they step through a hidden door, they enter a secret world without their parents to guide them. *Lord of the Flies* is also based on war events. In the book, an airplane full of evacuated families is shot down. They crash-land on an abandoned island. The only ones to survive are the kids. They try to build a society, but things don't go well. By the time they are rescued, they have started a war of their own.

World War II touched everyone. Even Michael, from his peaceful boyhood home in Reading, was called on to do his part. Many years later in 2009, Michael sent a message to children staying at the UK's Yarl's Wood Immigration Removal Center. He asked them to keep their hopes up while they waited for the government to decide whether they could remain in the country. Their plight reminded him how lucky he was to have lived freely in England.

Michael always remembered the children his parents took in for a short time. He never forgot the two boys so close to his age that stayed in his home. Recounting images of them looking forlorn made him sorrowful. The boys missed their parents so much that they rarely smiled. "They very sadly used to sit by the fire and cry," Michael said.

Not only were they glum, but they didn't get along with one another, which made things even more difficult. Michael tried to include them in neighborhood games of cricket, but often the older boy left the younger one in tears. *"Ich bin dran.* It's *my* turn," he would say in a bossy manner, snatching the stick to take a swing. When the younger boy took a crack at the wicket, the older one teased him about his wild swings.

"I was still a child myself, but mature enough to realize that what they were going through was awful," Bond said. Amidst all the turmoil they felt like outcasts, and Michael felt helpless as he tried to comfort them. Yet, without the assistance of his family, they may have been lost and homeless.

As fighting swept across the planet, Michael would learn more lessons. Not all of the lessons would be easy ones. Some of them would even put his life in danger.

Unbreakable

Michael spent his summers playing with Binkie and his pet guinea pigs. He also zoomed around Reading on his bike. When he ran into school-mates, they often played marbles for hours, until dusk set in and his rumbling stomach reminded him it was supper time.

Another popular kids' game was called conkers. Before anyone could play, they had to first make a conker, a chestnut seed hung from a piece of string. Lots of chestnut trees grew in the town's parks, so finding a large, strong seed was a fairly simple task.

But not every conker was good enough. It had to be fashioned cleverly, in the most indestructible way. The kids drilled a hole in the seed with something sharp, such as a nail. A piece of string was threaded through the hole, and a knot was tied at one end. Then the boys and girls took turns smashing their conkers into others' conkers. A point was scored when one seed broke the other seed.

"Do you want to go first?" Michael asked his friend.

"Yes," said his friend. "I bet my conker breaks yours right away!"

"I bet it doesn't."

He pinched one end of the string between his fingers and held out his arm. The seed dangled freely. His friend took aim and slung his seed. The conkers made a loud crack when they struck.

"My turn!" said Michael.

The other boy let his seed dangle. Michael swung his conker and whacked the other seed really hard. Both twirled madly, and the strings tangled. Whenever the strings snarled up like that, the first boy to shout out took a free turn.

"Stringsies!" Michael shouted.

His friend held out his conker. Michael landed another hard blow that split his friend's conker wide open.

"My conker has one point," Michael said. "Now it's a one-er."

"I'll have to make a new one," his friend said.

"The new one won't have scored any points," Michael reminded him. "So it will be a none-er!"

The two boys searched for another chestnut seed. Michael's friend wanted to find a good one, one that was unbreakable. They spent a lot of time sorting through seeds on the ground. While they were looking down, the sky swelled with rain clouds. Tiny droplets splashed the scattered chestnuts.

"Oh, I've got to go home," Michael said. "It's nearly time for supper."

"Can you come back later and finish the game?" his friend asked.

"I'll try." Michael hopped on his bike and waved goodbye.

When he skidded into his driveway, the tangy scent of fried onions drifted through the door. His mom had just finished making sausages and mashed potatoes.

"Bangers and mash!" Michael said. "Yum!"

His dad brought three plates piled high to the table. Then he tucked a napkin into his collar. As he cut into his sausage, he gave a little cough and looked over at Michael.

"You're going to start school soon," his father said.

"It will be great to see my friends every day," Michael said. "I really miss them when their families go on holiday."

"Well," said his mother, "this year you'll be able to make new friends."

His dad nodded. "We've decided to send you to Presentation College." Back then, British people used the word "college" to mean a high school.

"We want you to have a good education," his mother said. "Presentation College is an excellent private school."

Michael jabbed at his sausage with his fork. He had expected to hear stories of his father's mail delivery that day. Instead, this announcement had come as a surprise, and not a welcome one. "I don't much like school," he said. "The classes are boring."

"Give this a chance," his father said. "You are a smart boy, but you haven't applied yourself."

"Is it a Catholic school?" Michael asked.

"Yes," his mother said. "It's one of the best in the area. I picked it the moment I saw the uniforms. Wait until you see the jacket. It's a most lovely color!"

"It sounds even more boring than public school," Michael moaned.

Michael's dad shot him a look. Then his father forced a half-hearted smile and shook his head. It was best, Michael knew, not to say anything more. He would give the school a chance before he decided to hate it. He shrugged and popped a forkful of sausage into his mouth. He chewed it slowly, feeling it move past the knot in his throat as he swallowed. The news that he would be attending Presentation College had taken away his appetite.

The rest of the meal was spent discussing strategies for conkers. His dad had some great ideas for how to hit the seeds together just right. But the whole time they were talking, Michael couldn't stop thinking about his new school. He dreaded the end of summer, when it would be time to dress in an itchy tie and jacket every day. Just like those awful wool blankets.

● ● ● ● ●

On the first day of school, Michael discovered exactly how right he had been. His teacher was quick to punish his pupils. Back then, British educators were allowed to slap their students. They also used rubber straps and canes to swat them when they got into trouble.

To Michael, it seemed like any student who did the tiniest thing wrong suffered the headmaster's wrath. He watched the clock constantly, counting every minute until he could escape his classroom.

Sometimes Michael found ways to vanish while he was supposed to be in lessons. His favorite place to hide was in the bicycle shed. He became an expert at avoiding class this way. It was tempting to take a bike ride on the grassy length of the athletic field, snaking up and down the freshly mowed lines. When he heard his teacher calling for him, he ran back to the shed and concealed himself among the rows of rubber tires.

Although he was rarely punished for his disappearing act, Michael was occasionally spanked for laughing in class.

"Why did the chef get sent to prison?" Michael asked his classmate one day before school began.

"I don't know," his friend answered. "Tell me!"

"Because he beat the eggs and whipped the cream!" Michael attempted to muffle a giggle. Try as he might, he couldn't help cracking jokes. He loved to make the other students laugh. As soon as he told the punch line, his teacher walked in the room and gave him a sharp glare. The next thing he knew, he was hit with a switch, each blow stinging a little bit more than the one before.

It was hard for Michael to watch his friends be treated harshly, too. His mother and father had always been affectionate, and the aunties who were his caretakers taught him to be sensitive to others. Besides, he'd already witnessed thousands of frightened refugees flood into Reading.

Didn't many kids suffer enough already without getting scolded by teachers, too? This question haunted Michael.

The first chance he got, he stopped attending class altogether. Back then, children were allowed to leave school when they turned 12. Many students stopped going when they turned 13 or 14.

That's exactly what Michael did. He left Presentation College when he was 14 years old and, to his relief, he never returned. Although his teachers were proud when their former student became a famous author, Michael was glad to be gone from a place that held unhappy memories.

"My mother didn't make many mistakes in her life," Michael said. "But sending me to Presentation College was one of them."

● ● ● ● ●

Although Michael was finished with formal schooling, he wasted no time finding other ways to learn new things. Earning a wage meant a different kind of studying. With the older men off to war, work opportunities for teenagers were plentiful. For his first job, he filed legal papers in an attorney's office. When he turned 15, he began working for the British Broadcasting Corporation.

The BBC ran a wartime monitoring service out of Reading. The monitoring service, created in 1939, provided the government with news and reports from other countries. Keeping an eye out for propaganda was another service of the BBC. Too often, false information was used to mislead the public about the politics of war.

The building where Michael worked was called Caversham Park, and its property had a long history. William the Conqueror was given the estate in 1066 following the Norman conquest of England. When the house that stood on the estate burned down in 1850, it was replaced with an ornate structure modeled after an Italian baroque palace. The design was created by Horace Jones, the same architect who designed London's legendary Tower Bridge. By the time Michael started working, Caversham Park was an important center of information for the rest of Europe.

Inside the "palace" rooms, light poured in through towering windows. Journalists scoured reports pulled from newspapers around the globe. Long banks of radio equipment were used to monitor broadcasts. People who spoke different languages listened and translated for hours. Headphones covered their ears, so they sometimes talked over one another.

Michael loved the chaos and bustle. He worked beside people from every part of the world, and his technical skills were admired. Soon he was known as a "smart young man" who could repair almost anything.

"How did you learn so much about radios?" his manager asked.

Michael shrugged. "I build amplifiers at home. That way, my mother can listen to the radio shows she loves."

"Good boy," his manager said. "Can you fix anything else?"

"Sure!" Michael said. "I've taken apart almost every machine in our house."

"Taking them apart is one thing," his manager said. "Are you able to put them back together?"

"Every time!"

The man crossed his arms and leaned back. "Well, young Michael. How would you like to work at our transmitter facility?"

Transmitter facilities sent broadcasts out to radios and other devices. Every day, the broadcasts offered war reporting and music. The broadcasts also included shows that entertained American troops stationed in England.

"I would like that very much, sir," Michael said.

"Congratulations!" the manager said. "You've just been promoted to a junior job at the Reading facility."

"Thank you," Michael said. He hurried off to phone his mum the good news.

That same day, Michael was sent to the transmitter facility. At first the job went smoothly, and he kept the equipment in excellent shape.

Then, in a single instant, the work turned treacherous. On February 10, 1943, Michael was sent to the top of a building to fix the transmitter. The ground floor of the building housed the People's Pantry. Britain was rationing food again because of the war, and some families couldn't get enough to eat. They visited the People's Pantry to buy inexpensive meals.

As Michael stepped inside the building, he said hello to people he knew. After climbing the stairs all the way to the top, he stepped out onto the roof. The wind caught at his jacket. The day was cold, but hiking up all those stairs had warmed him up.

The sun was bright, and a peaceful sky boasted only a few, fluffy clouds. As Michael worked on the transmitter, he heard a strange sound over the wind. It was the loud buzz of a German plane. The air raid siren wailed.

People on the streets scurried for the nearest shelter. Most of them ran into the closest building. Others rushed to the holes they had dug in their gardens. For Michael, way up on the roof, no shelter could be found.

As Michael scanned the frantic scene, a plane called a Dornier dropped out of the clouds. The bomber had a thin body, so people call it the flying pencil. Machine guns mounted on its sides rained bullets onto the streets.

At the bottom of the plane was an open hatchway. Michael counted one, two, three, four bombs as they dropped from the hatch. Two of the bombs weighed 500 kilograms, or over 1,100 pounds. Each bomb was bigger than a grand piano!

The German air force made life hard for British people by destroying everyday places like bakeries and meeting places. One bomb took out a brewery and left a crater 25 feet across. Another bomb landed on a political office on Minster Street. A third hit a restaurant and damaged the town hall.

Then Michael watched the last bomb head straight toward the People's Pantry. He threw himself flat onto the roof and covered his head. The building shook as the bomb struck below him.

A terrible rumbling blotted out screams. The lower floors exploded in a cloud of dust. Just when Michael thought it was over, the building shuddered as part of the roof collapsed. Luckily, the portion where he lay stayed intact.

He pulled himself up and stumbled over to the stairway. One side of the structure was gone, and he could see sunlight cutting through the clouds of dust. Parts of the stairway were still there. He had to get down before the rest of the building caved in.

Michael placed each foot gingerly as he descended the steps. They shifted and groaned under his weight. When he reached each landing, he wriggled around furniture and chunks of brick. Finally, he arrived safely on the ground floor.

To escape the crumbling building, Michael scaled huge piles of rubble blocking the street. At first, the road appeared desolate. Wounded people were trapped under the weight of fallen bricks. Michael did what he could to dig them free. As he heaved aside debris, he could hear muffled cries of victims buried underneath.

Men and women, elderly people, and children had been hurt. Other people poured out of storefronts to help. Hours went by as rescue efforts continued. After the wounded had been taken to the hospital, there was nothing Michael could do but go home and assure his anxious parents he'd survived. A few blocks away, Michael found a bus waiting for stranded passengers.

"I got on the bus," Michael said, "but nobody sat near me. I was too dusty."

He didn't care about his disheveled appearance. He just wanted to make sure his mother and father were all right! When he arrived home, he was relieved to see they were unharmed. Minutes went by as the three of them held each other tightly.

More than 100 people were injured that day, and 41 died. Michael would never forget watching that plane drop those bombs. He would never forget the terrible price his neighbors paid—in lost homes and lives—during the war.

Voyages of Adventure

After surviving the bomb attack, Michael volunteered for the Royal Air Force. When he told his parents, they worried. Even so, they respected his decision.

"You are a good lad," his father said. "I want you to be careful, son."

His mother pulled a kerchief from her purse and sniffled. "You will make us proud," she said, dabbing her eyes. "You always do so much to help others."

"I will never forget how you took in those boys," Michael said. "The ones who came to live with us when I was 10. I need to make sure that everyone in England, including our refugees, remains safe here."

His mother began crying again. She was tearful, but also gratified that her son had grown into the kind of man who did the right thing. The lessons she'd taught him were still intact. She reached out and squeezed his hand.

"You will always be our little boy," she whispered. "You come home to us after this war is over."

He patted her shoulder softly. "I will, Mum. I promise."

As soon as Michael left home he reported to the flight training station. He was excited about joining the Royal Air Force. During those childhood visits with his aunties, he had watched many planes take off from Greenham Common Air Force Station. At last he would learn how to be a pilot.

The British government couldn't train all the people it needed for the war. On top of that, the weather in England was often foggy and rainy. Since it would be too difficult to train pilots there, the Allies offered to train RAF pilots in their countries, too. England sent trainees overseas to eight different countries to learn the basics of flight. In all, it took up to two years to become an air force pilot.

By the time Michael volunteered, over 300 flight training schools were operating around the world. Where would he be stationed? What new people would he meet? Which new places would he see? He couldn't wait to find out!

Despite his enthusiasm, Michael ran out of luck. For the first time in his life, he jumped into a plane. The test flight determined which of the recruits would go right into training. For Michael, the experiment went terribly wrong.

He was overcome with a severe case of airsickness. He was so ill that he couldn't focus on anything he was supposed to learn. His stomach churned as the flight instructor shouted commands. When the plane finally landed, Michael staggered off. His face was ghost white and beads of sweat dotted his forehead. He was so thankful to be on the ground again! Becoming a pilot was no longer a possibility.

The RAF gave him two choices. The first option was to leave the air force and become a coal miner. The government had purchased all the coal mines, so Michael could work in one of the pits. But the job was dirty and dangerous. The mines were also in rural villages thousands of miles from the bustling community Michael loved. The other choice was to transfer to the army. That would allow him to fight. If he couldn't do battle in the air, he would go into ground combat.

Michael joined the army's Middlesex Regiment, a group that specialized in machine guns. He was soon scheduled to go to Cairo, Egypt. Parts of North Africa had been invaded by Italian and German forces, so British troops were tasked with keeping control of the city.

Not only were Michael's parents unhappy to see him sent so far away, Michael too was hesitant to leave his friends behind. Before he departed, one of them gave him a gift.

"I want you to have this," she said. "Carry it with you all the time."

She handed Michael a small stuffed bear. The toys had become popular in 1902 after President Theodore "Teddy" Roosevelt went hunting and refused to shoot a cub.

Michael slipped it into his shirt pocket. When he was overseas, he would carry it everywhere to remind him of home.

• • • • •

Raymond Hare, a secretary at the US Embassy, said that Cairo, Egypt's largest city, was a mix of war and parties. Many times, servicemen went to a social affair knowing they would return to the desert to resume their duties early the next morning. They often relaxed at the officer's club still covered in soot because they had spent the day fighting.

Soldiers and ambassadors were not the only people sent to Cairo. Spies reported to the Office of Strategic Services, the early version of the Central Intelligence

Agency. Red Cross personnel provided food and medical care for civilians.

Just like Michael was in Egypt to serve his country, troops from other countries were stationed there, too. He welcomed every interaction with servicemen from distant lands. Whenever he went to the mess tent for a meal, he met people from places he'd never visited.

He also explored every corner of Cairo. Palm trees lined the streets. Signs were written in Arabic, which was read from right to left. Some of the army's tents had been set up near the pyramids at the outskirts of the city. Michael was amazed by these massive ancient tombs built with limestone bricks. Looking at them was like traveling back in time.

Other parts of the experience weren't so pleasant. British soldiers wore hot, heavy uniforms. The desert grew cold at night, so the clothing kept the men warm. But during the day, the temperature could top 90 degrees. The wool cloth was horribly uncomfortable in the heat. The soldiers dripped with sweat, but most days a cool shower was a luxury.

When Michael wasn't performing his duties, he sat on his cot and wrote. Maybe because his childhood had been spent with books, stories and articles flowed from his pen. Each one was folded and stuffed into an envelope. Whenever he sent off another piece of writing, he wondered if it would be published.

Finally, after many, many envelopes had been mailed, he received a response. *London Opinion* magazine bought one of his stories! Michael was paid seven guineas, which was an older type of British money. Today, those seven guineas would be worth about $500.

Michael thought that was a lot of money. He also thought, *I quite like the idea of being a writer.* Many more years would pass before his repeated attempts paid off.

● ● ● ● ●

Early in 1945, the Nazis were close to defeat. Their efforts at the bloody Battle of the Bulge and along the French-German border failed. Soviet and Polish forces pressured them out of East Prussia, and the Soviet Union agreed to join the war against Japan.

In April, Italian groups killed their tyrannical leader, Benito Mussolini. Two days later, Nazi leader Adolf Hitler killed himself in an air raid shelter in Berlin. German forces in different countries were weak and began to give up power. Japan surrendered on August 15. Finally, after too many years of fighting, the war ended on September 2, 1945.

During the war, around 60 million soldiers and civilians died. Ensuring peace was the only way life in Europe could get back to normal. Its many small nations needed to work together. In December 1946, Europe's borders changed. Land in the east was ruled by Poland and the Soviet Union. West Germany was formed by zones occupied by the United States, Britain, and France.

Nazi officials answered for unspeakable war crimes at the Nuremberg Trials. The soldiers who had spent so many months away from their families finally headed back home. Some had been wounded badly and would suffer the pain of their scars.

● ● ● ● ●

Michael Bond returned to the BBC to monitor the broadcasts from other nations. Even from Reading, he could connect with people from all over. He also worked alongside many Russian and Polish refugees who had fled to England. Each one of them brought a new perspective to Britain, adding more layers to daily life there.

While he worked as a cameraman, Michael kept writing. He finished dozens of short stories and a few plays. Although he mailed several pieces to magazines and newspapers, most of them were turned down. He failed more often than he succeeded.

"I could have pasted my room with rejection slips," he later said. "But I never gave up."

Fortunately, Michael's job was never boring. Back then, television programs were broadcast live, so everything happened at a fast pace. The crew had to pay very close attention to make sure everything ran smoothly. One small blunder could cost them an entire news day.

Eight years went by. Michael did his job so well that by age 22, he became a senior cameraman in charge of a crew. Then he was assigned to a children's show called *Blue Peter*. The name of the show caught his attention.

"That's an unusual name," Michael said to its producer. "Ships use a flag called a blue peter to tell people they are about to sail away from port."

"How did you know that?" the producer asked. It was a little-known fact for most people. "Do you own a boat?"

"I served in the military," Michael said. "I picked up things like that during active duty."

"Brilliant! A bright chap like you is just the kind of person we need behind the camera."

For this show, the blue peter flag represented an adventurous voyage for the children watching. Michael made sure the camera caught all kinds of action. Pets were often featured. One day Michael might have to film dogs and cats. The next, he filmed turtles and birds.

Some of those animals were not trained. They were often unruly and squirmed a lot. Joey, the *Blue Peter* parrot, squawked loudly while a pair of tortoises crawled among camera equipment. Mice and rabbits wriggled and scratched, making tunnels in their wood shavings. When it was time to fetch them, they were burrowed underneath. Meanwhile, Honey the guide dog sat patiently waiting for commands.

"There was always some disaster going on behind the scenes," Michael said. He was fond of animals, so their antics didn't faze him one bit. He calmly dealt with whatever chaos popped up in front of his lens.

Michael was also skilled at filming musicians and dancers who performed during the show. When the broadcast switched over to a prerecorded portion, Michael turned the camera off and on exactly at the right times. Even a one-second delay was considered a major mistake.

As his experience grew behind the scenes, Michael filmed many different shows aside from *Blue Peter*. One was *Dixon of Dock Green*, a fictional show about daily life in a London police station. He also worked on *Face to Face*, a personal interview program. Lord William Norman Birkett, who had been a judge for the Nuremberg Trials, conducted the interviews.

While Michael was crouched behind the camera, he looked out at the world with wide eyes. His curiosity about other people and how they lived never ceased. The camera lens framed real people who fed the stories and plays he filmed.

● ● ● ● ●

As Michael's career began to blossom, so did his brief courtship with his first wife, Brenda Mary Johnson. In 1950, the same year that Michael started his career as a cameraman, the couple married in a quiet ceremony.

Soon after their wedding, they moved in together in a tiny apartment in Maida Vale, London. Their one-bedroom flat was so small that Brenda and Michael compared it to "living in a caravan." They slept on a Murphy bed, a type of bed that folded up into the wall. In order to sleep, they first had to move furniture out of the way. At the time, "rag and bone" men, people who bought used goods to resell, rode horse-drawn buggies through the streets near their home. The wheels of their carts sounded like tap shoe dancers, as they clicked and rolled over paths of stone. News was still delivered over the radio, until a program in 1953 began to broadcast limited reports on television.

With the information he gathered about faraway people and places, Michael found continuous ways to learn. He chatted with neighbors who were immigrants from Hungary. He visited shops that sold goods from other regions. Today's world can be explored with a click of a mouse over the Internet. Back then, it took a lot more time and effort to study other cultures.

The BBC job was a perfect fit for such a curious man. As Michael worked his way up to senior cameraman, he kept writing. Even as the rejection slips piled up on his desk, he remembered his grandfather's words: "You can do anything, but you must keep trying."

Michael wrote story after story and article after article. When each piece was done, he stuffed it into an envelope and sent it out. A monsoon of rejection letters returned. He sold a manuscript now and then, but he couldn't seem to make a big sale that would allow him to write full time.

No matter what, Michael never gave up. His persistence would pay off in ways he had never dared imagine.

A Lonely Bear

O n Christmas Eve in 1956, Michael hurried home from work. The stores were closing early for the holiday. A few were still open, and shoppers hunting for last-minute gifts crowded the sidewalk.

When snow began to fall, Michael pulled his hat down low. He was wearing a duffle coat made from thick wool. Instead of buttons, the coat was closed using wood pegs called toggles. The coat had been made for soldiers, so it was rugged enough for him to wear when he filmed outdoor scenes.

That evening, a blizzard hit London. Michael didn't want to deal with the blustering storm, so he slowed his brisk pace and slipped into a store. Selfridges was a shop on Oxford Street close to Paddington Station. The building had been bombed during the war but had survived with only a little damage.

Michael dusted snowflakes from his felt cap and wandered through the store with the other shoppers. He waved off a few clerks who asked if he needed help. The shop was gigantic, so he hoped that he could walk around until the snow stopped.

Nine elevators and six staircases allowed customers to wander all five stories. Three basement levels reached 200 feet underground. The building was designed for 100 different departments. It was crowned by a rooftop terrace with gardens, cafes, and a miniature golf course. Those had been closed for decades after the building was damaged by bombs dropped during the war. Michael didn't miss the high-rise views. The weather was too frigid for a rooftop walk that day.

When he reached the toy department, he studied the dolls and games. He didn't have any children yet, but toys were always fun to look at. He stopped in front of a shelf that was nearly empty. Over to one side slumped a stuffed bear.

"Why, hello," Michael said. "You're up there all alone, aren't you?"

The shoppers had bought all the other bears. No one wanted this last one. It lay flopped over on its side, and its shiny eyes stared at him longingly. Being alone was

Shoppers outside Selfridges Department Store, London. *Anthony Baggett/Dreamstime*

not a happy way to spend the holidays. Michael picked up the bear and gave it a squeeze.

"You're perfect!" he said. "My wife will love you. Come on, then. We're going home."

He paid for the bear and stepped outside. The snow had let up a little bit, but he wanted to protect the toy. He remembered the stuffed bear he had kept tucked inside his uniform during the war. His coat made a fine nest for this new bear.

When he arrived at the tiny apartment, he handed the stuffed toy to Brenda. "I felt sorry for this bear," he said. "Fancy sitting on a shelf all by yourself over Christmas."

Brenda gave the bear a hug. "He will live with us," she said. She placed the toy on the fireplace mantle.

"What shall we name him?" Michael asked.

"Hmm," Brenda said. "Well, he has golden fur, so we could call him Honey."

Michael put a finger to his chin. "I'm afraid that's not quite right, dear. He is a dignified bear, and Honey is not a dignified name."

"Well, what do you propose?"

Michael thought back to his detour home to duck the snow. Selfridges was very close to Paddington Station, where he caught a train to work each day. He had long wanted to call one of his written characters Paddington because he liked the name so much.

Until now, he had never found the right character for that name. The title was unique, and reminded him of the trains that had fascinated him since he was a child. It needed a special, upright character to own it. This bear right in front of him fit perfectly.

"I think we should call him Paddington," Michael said.

Brenda clapped her hands. "What a delightful idea!"

"It's dignified," he said. "Just like our bear."

When they sat down to dinner that night, Michael glanced over at the fireplace.

"Do you suppose," he asked his wife, "that our new friend Paddington might like to join us?"

"For dinner?" Brenda asked.

"Yes." Michael nodded firmly. "Bears eat many things, you know. And this bear in particular loves food."

"He sounds like the perfect dinner companion," Brenda said. "Please do invite him."

Michael walked over to the mantle and bowed. "Paddington Bear, would you care to join us for dinner?" he asked.

"What did he say?" Brenda called from the kitchen.

"He said, 'Yes, thank you.'" Michael carried Paddington to the table and settled him in a chair of his own.

Brenda brought out their plates. When she set the food on the table, Michael leaned over the toy.

"Hmm?" he said. "What's that?"

He turned to Brenda. "Paddington says, 'Thank you for the lovely meal.'"

"What a polite bear!" she said.

"Of course," Michael said. "He minds his manners."

Soon the bear joined them when they ate at restaurants. Paddington always got his own chair. Other patrons must have been tickled to see the three of them eating together. Later, during Michael's frequent airplane travels, the bear would be invited up to the cockpit on every flight he took, though not because he could help the pilot navigate his aircraft. The crew wanted Paddington's company until they reached their destination.

Michael and Brenda both loved the bear's company. They were pleased to have him around to share their everyday lives. In Michael's opinion, bears had humanlike qualities, and Paddington was no exception.

"I think it's because they can stand on their back legs," he once explained.

The stuffed bear that had been rescued from an empty shelf at Selfridges also stood on its hind legs. And yet bears—let alone toy bears—clearly were not people. For Michael, they were somewhere in between.

The charming toy bear became their close friend. One day soon, Paddington would alter their lives forever.

● ● ● ● ●

Michael sighed heavily. Another rejection had arrived from another magazine. As hard as it was, Michael read every refusal, hoping for comments from the editor. Although he was happy that he and Brenda could afford a modest home with the income from his job as a cameraman, his dream was to support his family as a published author. Sometimes editors sent him short notes, offering suggestions to make his story better. These rare but encouraging words were what he needed to press on with his writing.

Most times, however, he was turned down with nothing more than a form letter. The only thing he could do was sit down at his desk, crank a fresh sheet of paper into his typewriter, and write something new. But where should he begin?

He could write an article about how the face of Britain had changed with the rise in immigration since the war. Hoping to fill an urgent need for workers, nearly 500 men came by ship from Jamaica. Many people from India and Pakistan had arrived in West London, where Michael lived, looking for labor. Eastern European evacuees who had fled the dangerous Nazi regime decided to stay, too. All day long, rushed exchanges in a symphony of languages rose above the busy city streets like musical notes. Michael listened closely to the tunes of many tongues on his way to work, relishing the stream of sounds that swept past his ears.

The number of immigrants had been climbing steadily for 20 years. Britain used to be called the British

Empire because they governed a lot of other countries and territories. The king of England even ruled the colonies that became the United States. England also held power in India until 1947, and ruled Hong Kong until 1997. Many people from these areas in Asia settled in the United Kingdom, too.

Michael's apartment stood right in the middle of this melting pot of people. On Portobello Road, he shopped at Notting Hill market. The Afro-Caribbean shops that lined the street offered stall after stall of foods from the West Indies. The salty, fresh aroma of goat stew wafted into his open window as he worked. As Michael's thoughts took shape, he tapped out a few words about the distinct talk and tastes of foreign cultures. Nothing seemed to take hold with that special spark a writer needs. He was too exasperated to think clearly, but giving up wasn't an option. Thankfully, he knew one man who always stayed calm. That man was Michael's literary agent, Harvey Unna.

Literary agents help writers sell their work to publishers. If anyone could help Michael out of this writer's block, it was Harvey. He was a Jewish refugee from Nazi Germany who would later inspire Paddington's good friend Mr. Gruber. When Michael phoned, they talked a bit about the mounting rejection letters. Then Michael took a deep breath. He was about to admit a frustrating thing for a man with a huge imagination. He needed to stay strong.

"Harvey, I just don't know what to write next. My mind is utterly blank."

Harvey didn't seem surprised or upset. Instead, he had an immediate reply.

"Describe your room," Harvey said.

"You want me to write about my room?" Michael asked.

Harvey laughed gently. "No, not exactly. Tell me what's in your room. Look around. What do you see?"

Michael scanned the objects around him. Since there wasn't space for a private office, he worked in the living room. The first thing he saw was the antique wall clock, then swiftly turned his sights to a framed picture of his parents on his desk. The black-and-white photo made them look more old-fashioned than Michael recalled. As he continued to look around, his eyes landed on Paddington.

"We have a small bear," Michael said.

"A bear?" Harvey asked.

"Yes," Michael said. "He is honey colored and has soft brown eyes. His name is Paddington."

"Write about that," Harvey said. "Write about Paddington Bear."

Michael hesitated for a moment. Then suddenly, he realized how wonderful the idea was!

"All right," he said. "I'll write about Paddington Bear."

He hung up and looked at the blank paper. Words seemed to swirl and dance on its empty page. Instead of noticing the typewriter beneath his fingertips, he saw an image of Paddington as a real bear. The young cub was standing on a train platform. Beside him sat a small suitcase that contained all of his belongings.

"How do you do?" Michael asked.

While he studied the scene in his mind, Michael pictured those refugee children from the war. They carried small suitcases with all their worldly possessions. They wore labels with their names around their necks. Perhaps Paddington was a refugee, too.

The only way to really find out was to start writing. Michael pecked out the letters that formed the first sentence. He wrote about a married couple, Mr. and Mrs. Brown, who met Paddington in the railway station. And, like the stuffed bear Michael had given to Brenda for Christmas, Mr. and Mrs. Brown named Paddington after the station.

"It was a simple act," Michael said about writing the first Paddington story. "The prose was not exactly earthshattering."

For the next several hours he remained frozen in his seat, typing furiously. Michael knew the story held promise. What he didn't know was that the simple words he typed on that paper were about to touch people everywhere.

All About Paddington

As Michael pressed the keys of his typewriter, he paused often to look at Paddington. So many questions spun in his head. Where did bears live? Why would a bear travel to London? Would the bear want to visit museums or would he want to find a new home?

Michael talked to Paddington Bear, who sat perched on the fireplace. While he wrote the first Paddington story, he asked questions of his stuffed companion. And for every question Michael asked, his imagination provided the answer.

"What kind of bear are you?" Michael wondered. After pondering it briefly, he guessed Paddington was an African bear.

"A bear from the wild bushlands of Africa!" He hammered out a few more sentences on his typewriter.

Then he looked up at Paddington. "But how did you get to Paddington Station?"

The stuffed bear looked a little forlorn.

"You might wonder whether I really want to hear your sad story," Michael said. "I do want to hear it."

He shifted around to face Paddington. He was about to say something important, and he wanted the bear to understand every word.

"The world is filled with grief," Michael said. "I have seen quite a bit of it in my life. Whatever sorrow you have felt, please share it with me. Sharing it might make you feel a bit better."

Paddington still seemed a bit gloomy. But he also looked a little hopeful, as if he might have found a friend who would understand.

"Ah, I see," Michael said. "Before you came to England, both your parents died."

He shook his head. "Heavens! How awful for you. How did they die?"

Was that a tear in Paddington's eye, or sunlight reflecting on its smooth glass surface?

"An earthquake, you say?" Michael asked. "Dreadful. They were both gone just like that."

Michael snapped his fingers. The ideas spilled from his head to his busy hands.

Paddington Railway Station, the first destination of the storybook bear. *Serban Enache/Dreamstime*

"How did you manage after your parents died?" he asked Paddington as he tapped on the keys. They creaked with wear. "Were you old enough to take care of yourself?"

Michael was lost in thought. Then all at once, he knew Paddington's aunt must have taken him in.

"Just like my aunties!" Michael said. "They were ever so kind. I understand what a comfort your Aunt Lucy must have been."

He quickly wrote another page of the story.

"Say," Michael asked, "how did you get from Africa to London? Bears can't swim that far, can they?"

He chuckled at his own foolishness. "Certainly not! You must have come over on a boat, like many other immigrants."

He stared at Paddington. The toy was small and cuddly, but a real bear would be much larger. It would frighten the passengers. The harbormaster would never have sold a ticket to a bear. Paddington must have found a different way to board the ship.

"You snuck onto the ship when no one was looking," Michael mused. "You were a stowaway! You tucked yourself into a lifeboat where no one would find you."

He pounded nonstop at the typewriter for the next 10 minutes. Finally, Michael took a break for more questions. "What did you eat? That was too long a journey to go without food."

Michael's brows creased. He thought about what a bear might eat during a sea voyage. Would he lean over the bow and scoop fish out of the water? No, someone would see him and scream in fright. Would he catch bugs and nibble on them every night? No, bugs couldn't fly far out over the ocean.

"A-ha!" he said. "You ate the food you had packed. What might fit in such a small suitcase? It must be something sweet, that bears like to eat. Perhaps a jar of orange marmalade!" Marmalade is jelly made from orange juice and peels. Michael knew he'd discovered Paddington's favorite, sticky meal.

The more Michael talked to Paddington, the more he learned that Paddington was a very brave bear. As it had been for many children of the war, courage was necessary for his survival. Michael recalled that Harvey, his literary agent, was once told his name was written on a foreboding list. Because Harvey was Jewish, he would be captured by the Nazis and shipped off to a concentration camp, where he would likely be killed. At the time, Harvey was about to become the youngest judge ever in Germany. But he swiftly fled to England instead, with just a suitcase and 25 pounds to his name.

That amount would be worth around $625 today— not enough for more than a few weeks of food and shelter. With so little money, finding a new home was hard. Michael thought about how lonely Harvey must have been with no friends to help out.

He also remembered the children who had showed up in Reading. The boy he met who held the gas mask had been happy about not having to go to school. Many of the other children had been scared. They missed their parents and friends and struggled to remain in contact with them. Their hopes for a happy reunion quickly dwindled as the days and weeks went by.

"So," Michael murmured to Paddington. "You also would have been lonely when you showed up in London. And you certainly would have shivered. The climate here is much different than in Africa."

To solve this problem, Michael gave his character a warm, blue coat. In fact, it was the same type of duffle coat Michael wore to work every day. To keep the bear's head warm, he gave Paddington a bright red hat. Exactly like the one Michael wore when he rode his motor scooter.

For 10 days straight, Michael sat at that typewriter and tapped out one word after another. Whenever he got stuck, he asked the stuffed bear a few more questions. He learned that Paddington was polite, and that most times, his good manners helped him do things the right way.

Because he was a stranger to the city of London, Paddington made a lot of mistakes, but every misstep taught him something new. Mr. Gruber, the Hungarian antique shop owner Paddington befriended, also gave helpful advice. The two enjoyed their "elevenses" together—a midday snack, often consisting of hot cocoa and chocolate buns, where Mr. Gruber offered his wisdom as an older refugee. Not everyone Paddington encountered cared about kindness, however. Those people always received a hard stare that made them blush from embarrassment for their rude behavior.

"Who taught you that neat little trick?" Michael wondered. "I know! Your Aunt Lucy taught you that."

Finally, after all that waiting and wondering and tapping away at the typewriter keys, the story was finished. Michael packaged it up and mailed it off to his agent.

"It was the first time I had written for children," Michael once said. "But I didn't have the age of my readers in mind. I was writing it for myself."

As the story of Paddington Bear unfolded in many more books, Michael would discover more about this loveable little bear. Along the way, Paddington would also become Michael's moral compass. But before any of that could happen, the first book he bashed out in only a week and a half had to be bought by a publisher. How many rejection slips would Michael receive this time?

$$\bullet \quad \bullet \quad \bullet \quad \bullet \quad \bullet$$

For over a month, Michael waited to hear from his agent. Every time he got home, he asked Brenda if the phone had rung. She was pregnant, and Michael worried that she wouldn't be able to reach it quickly enough.

"Stop your fretting," she said. "I am never far from the phone. I always pick up before the caller hangs up."

"So, then?" Michael asked. "Did Harvey call?"

"Not yet, love," she said. "I'm sure he will call soon."

Michael continued to worry. What would Harvey think of the story? Would he be upset that the story was for children? Would he know any publishers who were interested in children's books?

The waiting was endless. Then, just as Michael and Brenda were sitting down for dinner one evening, the telephone rang. Michael jumped from his chair and snatched the receiver.

"Hello?" he said. "Hello? Can you hear me?"

"I can hear you just fine," Harvey said.

Michael was bursting with anticipation to hear Harvey's thoughts about the story. But being rude was out of the question. So, he first asked how Harvey was doing, and they chatted a bit about Brenda. Finally, at long last, Harvey cleared his throat.

"Well, then. About this story," Harvey began.

"You mean *A Bear Called Paddington*," Michael said.

"Yes, *Paddington*," Harvey said. "There is a slight problem."

Disaster! Michael glanced at the stuffed bear on the mantle. What could be wrong? Perhaps Harvey didn't like bears. Maybe publishers would think that Michael was trying to copy *Winnie-the-Pooh*. A million earthquakes shook his thoughts.

"What might the problem be?" Michael asked.

"There are no bears in Africa," Harvey said. "At least, not today. The Atlas bear used to live there, but the last one died in 1870."

"I see." Harvey was always full of facts that got right to the point.

Michael glanced at Brenda. She was watching him carefully. She could tell that something was wrong, but she couldn't hear Harvey's voice.

"Well, then," Michael said. "Perhaps Paddington comes from a different country. A place that still has bears."

"Changing that would be a wise choice," Harvey said.

"Otherwise," Michael said, "did you like the story?"

"Very much!" Harvey said. "I think we have a real chance at getting this published."

"You don't know how happy that makes me!" Michael said.

Brenda grabbed her round belly and gave it a pat. She didn't know exactly why her husband was happy, but it had to do with his writing. The news must be good.

Harvey made a few more suggestions and told Michael to send him a fresh copy after he had made the changes. The moment Michael hung up, he celebrated with his wife. Right after dinner, he went back to the typewriter to work up a new version of *A Bear Called Paddington*.

This time around, Paddington became a Peruvian spectacled bear. The spectacled bear is closely related to the Florida spectacled bear, which lived in North America long ago. The spectacled bear is the only species of bear native to South America. Although it is a carnivore, or meat eater, it eats very little meat. That fit right in with Michael's story of a kindhearted bear that loved marmalade.

But the bear's fur is most often black, with a tan face framed by black patches. That didn't fit Michael's character at all. He pictured Paddington as the same color as his stuffed bear. However, some spectacled bears are light brown, while others have a reddish tint. Paddington could be tan, just like Michael had imagined.

Everything seemed to be falling into place for Michael and Paddington Bear. Then Harvey sent the story to publishers. Time after time, the publishers read the story and said no. The rejection slips piled up again, seven in total. Michael could only worry, and anxiously await more responses.

He often skipped sleep to sit at his typewriter. A few minutes here, an hour there, were stolen from his days. After all, his grandfather had said to never give up! One day, Michael knew, he would make it as a writer. Finally, his agent called again.

"Michael," Harvey said, "Collins wants to buy your book."

"That's great news!" Michael said, jumping up from his desk chair. "William Collins publishing house has been around for a while, hasn't it?"

Paddington Bear UK stamp, featuring an illustration by Peggy Fortnum, the first artist to draw the fictitious bear. *Chris Dorney/Dreamstime*

"Over 100 years," Harvey said. "And the deal is fair. Are you ready to hear this?"

Michael held his breath. He managed to say, "Yes."

"Collins is offering 75 pounds for the story," Harvey said.

That would be worth nearly $2,300 today.

"Sold!" Michael said.

After the contract was signed, things moved quickly. Peggy Fortnum, an illustrator, was hired to draw the pictures. The book was published in 1958—the same year Brenda gave birth to their first child, a daughter they named Karen. That brought a lot of joy to their crowded apartment. Between helping Brenda with the baby and working, Michael was busier than ever.

Life with Paddington

The moment Michael sold his first Paddington story, his life changed. The book was quickly named "Best Children's Novel" by the UK book trade journal, *Books and Bookmen. More About Paddington,* Michael's second novel, was published in September 1959.

Even before the bear's popularity soared, Paddington was part of Michael's days. No matter where Michael went, he thought about how the bear might experience London.

Portobello Road had always been Michael's favorite street to explore. The shops were on the lowest floor of the townhomes that lined the streets. The owners lived on the upper floors, and the fronts were painted in a rainbow of pastel colors. Sky-blue and sunny-yellow houses stood next to mint-green ones. A rosy-pink home might be next to a coral-orange house.

Michael discovered a perfect place for Paddington to seek adventure. It was a supermarket. The idea of having lots of things for sale inside a single building was new at the time. All kinds of wares from soda pop to broomsticks were sold in one place. The actual supermarket Paddington Bear visits in his books remains open in London today.

Even though grocery stores were just becoming popular, Michael and his neighbors still bought most of

Busy Saturday at Portobello Market, London. *Baloncici/Dreamstime*

their food from booths set up on the streets. The vendors carried the freshest vegetables and fruits. Michael and Brenda browsed the rows with their young daughter, inspecting crisp, scarlet apples and carrot bunches pulled straight from the ground. Most people didn't own refrigerators yet, so they only got the food they needed for each day's meals.

"My, those oranges look lovely!" Brenda said, picking up the plump, ripe fruit.

"Shall we get some?" Michael asked.

"Yes, please."

Michael turned to the woman at the booth. "One eighth bushel of oranges, please." That was around five pounds.

"That's quite a bit of oranges, luv," the vendor said as she filled a paper sack. "Is the misses making marmalade?"

Brenda laughed. "Heavens, no. I have no time for making jam now that I have a child."

"But you have to keep Paddington fed." The vendor winked. These days, most folks in West London recognized Michael, who was by now a famous writer.

Michael took the bag of oranges. "Indeed, we do. Not to worry. Paddington eats with us every evening. He is a well-fed bear."

"I worry about you sometimes," the vendor said jokingly. "You talk about that bear as if he were your child."

"But he is like my child," he said. "And my friend."

"Well," the vendor said, "I suppose you *have* brought him to life."

Karen, who was seven at the time, listened intently to the entire conversation. She knew it wasn't polite to interrupt adults. But she couldn't stay silent any longer.

"Paddington is real!" she exclaimed.

The vendor's eyes softened and she smiled. "So, little one, are you scared of your brother bear?"

"No," Karen said, "not one bit. Paddington is fuzzy and sweet and kind. And he's taller than me!"

"He's about this high," Michael said, his hand hovered over his daughter's head.

The vendor covered her mouth to keep from giggling. She was amused by the way the Bonds treated Paddington like another family member. She held up one finger so that the group of them would wait. She dipped under the table and rummaged around in a box. When she stood back up, she handed Karen a small jar of marmalade.

"You give that to Paddington Bear for me," said the vendor. "I know how much he likes it."

"Thank you, ma'am!" Karen said.

Michael and his family, including Paddington Bear, walked farther down Portobello Road. Karen was quiet for a very long time.

"Papa, would your mum and dad have thought Paddington was real?" Karen asked. Her grandparents were gone now. Although she knew it made her father sad to think about, she needed to know the answer.

"They would have known he was real," Michael said.

"What would they have done if they had met him?" she asked.

"My mother wouldn't have been able to resist his charm," he said. "She would have taken him in and given him a home."

"Would you have liked that?" she asked.

"Yes, very much," he said wistfully.

"What about your father?" she continued. "Would he have liked Paddington?"

"Well," Michael said, "my father was a civil servant to the ends of his fingertips. He probably would have worried that taking in a bear wasn't exactly allowed by the officials."

"So, he would have let Paddington live on the street?" Karen asked.

"Heavens, no! My dad would have helped. He always assisted people in trouble. Do you remember the two boys I told you about?"

"You mean the ones who ran away from the bad soldiers during the war?"

"Yes. My father took them in. If he had known that a sweet bear was wandering around without a home, he would have opened the door to Paddington and invited him in."

"For tea?"

"And a whole lot of marmalade, too." Michael leaned down, wrapped his arms around Karen and scooped her up in a big hug.

Karen smiled with delight as her father gently set her down. Then she reached over and took the hand of the invisible Paddington Bear. Michael took Paddington's other invisible hand and offered Brenda his arm. Together, the four of them strolled down Portobello Road, looking for the next big story idea for their best friend Paddington.

● ● ● ● ●

Soon after *A Bear Called Paddington* was released, Michael's loveable cub had a loyal following. Kids couldn't get enough of Paddington's innocent stumbles, and Michael didn't want to disappoint them by keeping them waiting. In 1965, six books later and seven years after the first story came out, Michael was able to quit his job as a cameraman. His parents had been worried he couldn't make a proper living writing children's books. By the time he left the BBC, he had proven that wrong.

Finally, Michael could live his dream and write all the time. Success didn't change him at all. He never lost his sense of humor. Even when he left the BBC, he did it in a fun-loving way. He gave up his job on April Fool's Day.

By 1972, Paddington Bear was a runaway success. Michael wrote three more books after quitting his cameraman job. Sales of the stories were climbing and showed no signs of slowing down. Since Paddington was in such high demand, a toy company called Gabrielle Designs wanted to make a stuffed bear based on the character. Shirley Clarkson, who had started the company out of her home in Doncaster in the northern part of England, knew a plush Paddington would make the perfect companion for kids.

The first products she sold were not stuffed bears, but tea cozies. The colorful cloth bags were tucked over teapots to keep the drink warm. The ones she made turned the teapot into what looked like a rooster. When they sold well, Shirley's creativity expanded into making aprons and lampshades.

Although she loved sewing practical items, she kept coming back to the idea of Paddington Bear. Her two children had introduced her to the books. They agreed that designing a cuddly plush cub was a brilliant idea. After flipping through pages again and again, Shirley decided to make a stuffed bear that looked just like the storybook character.

Using square swaths of soft, furlike cloth, she sewed a honey-colored bear. She gave it shiny dark eyes and a cute, black nose. Since Paddington walked on his hind legs in the drawings, the stuffed bear stood up too.

Then she stitched his outfit. The trench coat was made of a felted material with a wool appearance. The coat had toggles to hold it closed. A floppy hat of red material topped the toy.

"There," Shirley said, as she put the finishing touches on Paddington. "This is going to be a big hit!"

By the time the first bear was finished, Christmas had arrived. Paddington waited patiently under the tree on Christmas morning. Shirley's son Jeremy, who would grow up to become host of the car show *Top Gear*, was 12 at the time. He clapped his hands and hugged the toy tightly.

He and his sister spent hours playing with Paddington. For weeks, Jeremy and Joanna conjured up adventures for the stuffed bear. Shirley knew producing the toy in larger quantities was a must. Only her company would understand the passion it took to design such a precise replica of the bear from darkest Peru.

Shirley made a few phone calls. She tracked down Michael's lawyers and started negotiating with them to allow her to produce toy Paddingtons. Michael adored the plush bear, and Gabrielle Designs got the job. The first bears were made by hand in a small factory. In fact, the factory stitched so many Paddingtons that it became known as Bear Garden.

Each toy looked exactly like the prototype Michael approved. But as soon as the bears were ready to ship to stores, a problem came up. In the storybooks, Paddington stood on his hind legs, but the toys couldn't stand up on their own.

Shirley found a solution that would become part of Paddington forever. She bought a set of wellingtons, tall rubber boots named after the first Duke of Wellington, Arthur Wellesley. She purchased the smallest pair she could find, a child's size, and tested them on the plush toy.

The boots worked perfectly. The soles were heavy enough to keep Paddington from toppling over, and the bear looked even more likeable with the boots. Later, Shirley designed pajamas, a robe, and duffel coats in different colors. There were even rugby outfits, lace-up sneakers, and Paddington-sized gym bags.

Soon the toy bears were everywhere. People bought so many that the boot company couldn't make enough

Original Paddington Bear soft toy, made by Gabrielle Designs.
David J. Green/Alamy Stock Photo

wellingtons. Shirley again used her imagination to figure out how Bear Garden could make tiny rubber galoshes. And because the boots were for Paddington, she molded paw prints onto the soles.

● ● ● ● ●

In 1975, the BBC broadcast the very first Paddington Bear television show. Michael wrote the script himself. The show was animated through a technique called stop-motion. For this type of film, a Paddington puppet was placed on a tiny stage set.

The other characters were all paper cutouts. The puppet and the cutouts were moved one small step at a time. Photographs were taken of the characters in the different poses. Then the photographs were run together to create a film. The process took a lot of time.

The show quickly gained a large audience. Paddington fever grew so strong that people couldn't get enough of the bear. Dishonest companies made illegal copies of the plush toy. An ad put out by Gabrielle Designs told people how to tell if a Paddington toy was real. The fakes, the advertisement said, were "often ill-fed and ill-clothed."

Shirley was worried about the low quality of the fake bears. She didn't want anything to interfere with the joy

Paddington brought to children. Besides, it was illegal since Michael hadn't given permission to create those toys. To make her point, she wrote a humorous advertisement. The ad read, "Please don't try to take the marmalade out of Paddington's sandwiches!"

Stand selling dozens of official Paddington Bear stuffed toys in Paddington Station. *Marc-andre Le Torneux/Dreamstime*

In 1978, 87,000 Paddington plush bears were sold. The marmalade stayed inside Paddington's sandwich, and the money rightfully remained inside Shirley and Michael's pockets.

Paddington Bear
Rescues Mr. Bond

Work, work, work. As much as Michael relished writing about Paddington Bear, the job never seemed to end. The television show had made the books more popular than before. Contracts were sent to him constantly from television producers. His publisher asked for more manuscripts. To meet the demand, Michael wrote a new Paddington book almost every year.

He also started writing a new series with a different cast of characters. This one was about a guinea pig named Olga da Polga. Although most of her days were quiet, Olga spun tall tales out of ordinary events. Her

friends included a cat, a tortoise, a hedgehog, two ham-
sters, and a toad.

The series never sold as well as Paddington's books.
But Michael enjoyed writing about the guinea pig, so he
continued to write one of Olga's books every few years.

"Michael," Brenda often said to him over dinner.
"You're working much too hard."

"I know," he said.

"You are writing before the sun comes up," she said.

Karen looked up from her meal. "And you don't finish until after I'm asleep. I want to see you more often,
Pops."

Michael felt hopeless. "What more can I do? I need
to take care of my readers. They love Paddington Bear."

"And I love you," Karen pleaded.

He stared at her for a long moment. Then he crum-
pled up his napkin and laid it beside his plate.

"You haven't finished your meal," Brenda said.

"This is more important," Michael said. "I have an
idea."

Karen knew that when her dad had an idea, it was
certain to be an unusual one. Maybe he could fix their
problem and still keep his readers happy.

Michael checked the day's paper. England's cricket
win over Pakistan dominated the headlines. Although his
father was a sports trivia whiz, Michael never had much

interest in athletics. He flipped through the pages until he found the article he remembered reading that morning.

"Look here." He took the paper back to the table, and spread it out in front of them. "There's a fairly new neighborhood in London. It's called the Barbican Estate."

"Oh," Brenda said. "I might have heard about that."

"Aren't they building a library there, too?" Karen asked.

"Yes," Michael said. "And a museum, and a school for girls."

"And a music school!" Karen said.

"A lot of apartments are available." He pointed at a picture of the high-rise towers.

"Can we live up really high?" she asked.

"Perhaps," he said. "If we do find an apartment on an upper floor, we can pretend that we are in the old Roman watchtower that used to be there."

"But Michael," Brenda protested. She wasn't convinced this plan was the answer to their problem. "Why would we want to move? This place is perfectly fine."

"It has everything we need right there," he said. "I'll have more time to spend with you both."

He reached across the table to take his daughter's hand. "My father always used to say that the best thing you can give your child is your time," he said. "I haven't given you nearly enough. That's going to change."

The family found a new apartment they liked in Barbican Estate and moved in. Michael's home was now closer to his agent and publisher, but he was still under a huge amount of pressure. Hundreds of letters arrived every week from children around the world. Like always, he vowed to read them all and write new books.

Michael gave interviews to television shows and newspapers around the clock. He worked with the toy company to approve designs for different Paddington products. The bear had become a hugely successful brand, like Peter Rabbit. And he was writing scripts for the television show. Day after day, the business of bears consumed him.

No matter how hard Michael tried, he still didn't have enough time to do it all. He was working 18 hours a day. He disappeared during family dinners, eating at his desk instead. Living with Michael was like living with a ghost, and his relationship with Brenda crumbled. Karen adored her father, so she forgave his constant absence, but Michael couldn't forgive himself. Even when Michael wrote for 12 hours a day, he felt like it wasn't enough. He fell into a depression that lasted for two long years.

Every day looked and felt like all the other days. Michael rushed here, and he ran there. He wrote another story and called his agent. He agreed to more interviews and turned in countless television scripts. In between, he struggled to find time to spend with his wife and daughter.

Although the family had changed addresses, nothing else had changed. Their perch inside the Barbican Estate wasn't helping Michael escape from his stress. The only thing he could count on was more work and more obligations.

That is, except for one nice thing that always lifted his spirits: all those letters from children and parents that poured into Michael's office! They covered his desk to the point that he could barely find his own manuscript pages. Every day, Michael read a new message from a child who loved Paddington Bear. Many of the letters said that Paddington had brightened their lives. Some of the people who sent correspondence were immigrants and refugees. Paddington's familiar escapades helped them feel a little less homesick in their new country.

The storybook bear's troubles made them more accepting of their own blunders. Slowly, Michael began to realize that kids and adults across the globe counted on Paddington. The bear's innocence and persistence encouraged readers to keep trying their best. For millions of people, Paddington was more than just a fictional character.

That was something worth changing his ways for. Michael had a responsibility to Paddington, and to the

Paddington Bear migration poster appearing in Great Britain. *Gruffydd Thomas/Alamy Stock Photo*

kids who relied on the bear as much as he did. The only way he could meet that task was to be there for those he cherished most. Of course, that included Paddington Bear.

"There is something so upright about Paddington," Michael said. "I wouldn't want to let him down."

Michael was renewed. He found his old sense of humor. Even though he and Brenda eventually divorced after 31 years of marriage, they remained good friends and happiness returned to his life. He and Brenda even took turns keeping the original stuffed bear. After their separation, Michael said, "We ring each other and say, 'He feels like coming to you now.' I wouldn't go on holiday without him."

In 1981, Michael met his second wife, Susan Rogers. She answered the phones at his agent's office. He liked her voice but was too nervous to invite her out on a date. Instead, he asked her if she wanted to see a Paddington play.

Life took on a whole new spark. The dark cloud of depression was lifted, and Michael was thankful his readers had stood by him when his outlook was grim. In the first book, the Brown family rescued Paddington Bear from a railway station. Many books later, Paddington Bear rescued Michael Bond.

• • • • •

After Michael married Susan, they moved to Haslemere, Surrey, southwest of London. Haslemere was a much smaller town than other places Michael had lived. The quiet lifestyle allowed him to relax.

The best part of Haslemere might have been the railway station. The building had only two platforms, so it wasn't as grand as Waterloo Station in London. Even so, it was a good place to view massive locomotives transporting passengers to and fro. At certain times of day, Michael could stop by and watch the South Western Railway trains pass through. During those stretches of time he felt like a young boy again, awestruck by the engine's powerful roar.

Every two years, the town's Charter Fair took over the main street. Charter fairs are events established by a historical decree, dating back as far as the Middle Ages. Though he missed big city life, Michael enjoyed the Charter Fair and all its oddities. He didn't have to go farther than High Street to see curiosities of all kinds. Visitors came from everywhere to gorge themselves on slices of pie, washed down with pints of sweet cider. They sifted through handmade rugs and woolen sweaters, and bartered for wares with the busy merchants. Jugglers and flute players added a merry backdrop to the bedlam. When the week finally ended, the crowd dispersed and serenity settled in again.

Michael's new address in Surrey was a surprise to his readers. Many fans traveled to London to find Paddington's home. But the house at 32 Windsor Gardens in Notting Hill didn't exist, except in the books. Michael had mixed his parent's address in Reading with the address of his old apartment.

Some of his fans would not be discouraged. Rather than heading out to see other tourist sights, they traveled to Surrey, walked through the village, and knocked on Michael's door. If they clutched a Paddington Bear toy or book, he knew exactly why they had come. He treated them with the same politeness Paddington always offered.

"Hello," Michael said to a man standing on his front porch. "How may I help you?"

"You're Michael Bond!" the man said.

"So I'm told." Michael smiled.

"I'm so sorry to bother you," the man said.

"Rubbish! No bother at all. Won't you come in?"

The man froze. The last thing he had expected was for the great Michael Bond to ask him inside.

"Come in," Michael repeated. "Would you care for a cup of tea?"

"Oh, yes, please," the man replied.

No matter how many fans showed up at Michael's door, he always treated them as if they were his friends. He chatted with them over tea and autographed the books they carried. Michael always said he was shy, so this was another way Paddington helped him.

When he wrote about Paddington, he felt as if he were writing about a more confident part of himself. The bear had many adventures and craved meeting new people. Through Paddington, Michael experienced things he would have been too bashful to do himself.

"Unless an author believes in his character," Michael said, "no one else is going to. Paddington isn't me, but I wouldn't mind being him."

In some ways, Michael was Paddington Bear. In other ways, Paddington Bear was Michael. Together, the fictional character and the writer were an ideal twosome. They both spread a lot of joy, and it was doubly returned to them.

●　●　●　●　●

Many years later, Michael and Susan moved back to London. Their new neighborhood was called Little Venice. A canal ran through the area and houses lined the water. Houseboats painted in bright hues were tied up on both banks.

Early every morning, Michael left his house to visit Paddington Station. A bear-shaped box had been set up there to collect donations for charities. Next to the box stood a glass case filled with Paddington Bear plush toys.

By then, Gabrielle Designs had created a sitting version of the stuffed bear. Many of the others still stood on their hind legs. Crowds of people bumped the glass case so often that the standing bears fell over.

Though no one had asked him to, Michael took care of tidying the display. He opened up the case and propped all the bears back up. Then he rearranged the bears to make sure they looked good. He wiped everything down to make it shiny and clean, and he checked the lock on the charity box.

As people passed by, they recognized him. Some stopped to talk about his books. If they had children along, they introduced their kids to Michael. It was

Canals of London's Little Venice neighborhood. *Giuseppe De Filippo/ Dreamstime*

exciting to run into a famous author on the way to work or school!

In 2000, the glass case was replaced with a bronze statue of Paddington Bear. The statue shows Paddington sitting on his small suitcase and looking over his shoulder. His gaze falls on the railroad tracks. He watches the trains come in just like Michael did when he was a young boy.

Bronze statue of Paddington Bear at Paddington Station. *Alja Lehtonen/Dreamstime*

Paddington Lives On

For many years after Paddington became a household name, Michael continued to live and work in West London with his wife Susan. Every morning, he got dressed and prepared for his writing. He often stopped in the hallway to look at their paintings of French landscapes. In the past, he'd spent a month every year in Paris. He found it was a peaceful place to write, away from the hubbub of his London home.

"Do you think we'll ever get back to France?" his wife asked one day.

"I don't think so, love," Michael said. "My health isn't as good as it was when I was 80."

"You always say that you're *only* 91," Susan said.

"Yes, I am only 91," he said. "That doesn't stop me from working every day. But it does make travel difficult."

"You so loved your road trips across France," she said.

Michael smiled as he remembered the happy times they'd spent traveling. "We always ended our trip at the Cannes Film Festival," he said. "It was such a wonderful party."

"I enjoyed seeing the stunning gowns the actresses wore," Susan said. "They all looked so glamourous."

Michael touched the sleeve of her robe. "I think you are lovely in this!"

She blushed and patted his cheek. "You are always such a gentleman."

"Thank you, my dear."

He moved slowly down the steps. The lower level of his home had a large dining room where he kept two guinea pigs. He opened their cage door and shook food into their bowl. They gobbled up the kibble and sniffed at his fingers. He scratched their fat necks.

"Who wants to be first today?" Michael teased. "Ah, Olga. Always ready to go."

Using both hands, he gently cupped Olga and took her out of the cage. Cradling her wriggling body against his chest, he moved past the table. After setting her free on the floor, he returned to the cage for the second guinea pig.

"Up you go, Oksana," he crooned.

He placed Oksana on the floor next to Olga. The two wasted no time exploring the room. The dining room had a door, but just like the one to his childhood bedroom, it always remained closed so that they couldn't get into trouble.

Michael moved to his desk and settled in front of his computer screen. "I just press a button," he said to himself, recalling thousands of hours spent in front of a typewriter. "The words appear on the screen, and off I go."

With a computer, he didn't have to pound on the keys. His fingers didn't grow tired, so he could work as long as he liked. That wasn't always a good thing, but to Michael it was a luxury.

As soon as he sat down, Susan popped her head through the door.

"Michael, can you take some time off today?" she asked, "I'd like us to go for a walk."

"I work seven days a week dear," he said. "I wouldn't feel quite myself without writing."

"I know," she said. "It's just that the weather is so nice. We shouldn't miss it by staying inside."

"You're right, as always," he said. Nine times out of ten, England's summer days required an umbrella. "Let me finish this sentence, and we'll go out."

Though she knew one sentence would turn into paragraphs and then pages, Michael's answer satisfied Susan.

She left him with his morning thoughts. Patience was important in a good marriage.

"I can't think what I would do if I didn't write," he said out loud, taking a small sip from a steaming cup of tea. "Making up stories is never a grumble."

Michael couldn't complain. Not in his wildest dreams had he imagined Paddington would be so popular. He cherished every moment he spent writing about the bear's adventures. The 150 Paddington books he'd written had been translated into 40 different languages. There was even a version in Latin. In the nearly 60 years since he'd begun the series, 35 million copies had been sold. When the Channel Tunnel linking Britain and France was completed in 1994, a Paddington Bear stuffed toy was the first thing to pass through.

A few short years before—nearly half a century since *A Bear Called Paddington* was first published—Hollywood approached Michael about making a movie based on his books. The first Paddington film, released in 2014, was a triumph. Its producer, David Heyman, had also masterminded the Harry Potter motion pictures. Much to his delight, Michael played a small role in the Paddington movie. The short cameo cast him as a character known as the Kindly Gentleman. In this particular scene, Paddington had just reached London alone. The Brown family took him home in a taxi. The Kindly Gentleman

Paddington movie DVD cover. *Allstar Picture Library/Alamy Stock Photo*

was seated at the window of a restaurant and, as the taxi zipped past, raised his glass to the bear.

Being on set reminded Michael of his years as a cameraman at the BBC. Though the equipment was more technical now, the production process was familiar, and he was thrilled with the way the movie turned out. In fact, he described it as "magical." Three years later in 2017, *Paddington 2* arrived to rave reviews. Best of all, the films brought the bear to life. Now others could feel how real Paddington was, too!

● ● ● ● ●

After Michael had been writing away for a few hours, Susan returned to the doorway.

"Really, dear," she said. "You're working yourself to death."

"I don't worry about death," he said. "I am an old man. Not many can say they've reached 91."

"Then come with me for that walk you promised."

He saved the file and logged off the computer. As he stood up, he stretched. His back ached a lot, but he didn't let the pain stop him from doing most of the things he wanted to do. Taking Susan's arm, they strolled out onto the sidewalk. Like its counterpart in Italy, Little Venice was interspersed with canals. He and Susan often took scenic, water-lined walks, passing quaint pubs and restaurants on their leisurely journey.

Michael said nothing at first. Since the movie had come out, he'd been thinking more about Paddington's future. He knew his daughter's passion for the bear was as true as his own. In fact, Karen now ran Paddington and Company, a merchandising firm. After a minute or two of silence, he shared his thoughts with Susan.

"Paddington has been with me for 60 years," he said. "That's a very long time."

"He's been your true friend," Susan said.

"Do you suppose Karen might like to work on the books after I'm gone?" he asked.

"I am certain she will," she said. "She often talks about the ways she can manage the stories. Maybe she'll add a few of her own, too."

"She will keep Paddington Bear alive. That makes me so pleased."

"Paddington will live forever in the hearts of his readers," Susan reassured him.

The couple continued their stroll in silence, occasionally peeking into the shop windows along their route. Many displays starred at least one Paddington Bear. For six decades, the world had embraced Paddington. All because Michael had never given up on his dream of being a writer.

Paddington pop-up shop, celebrating 60 years since the publication of *A Bear Called Paddington*. *Alena Kravchenko/Dreamstime*

• • • • •

In April 2017, Michael's last book, titled *Paddington's Finest Hour*, was published. In the book, Paddington's troubles include a run-in with police, who question his immigration status. Just two months later, on June 27, Michael Bond died at age 91. Fans from around the world sent letters and cards to his family. When his daughter Karen stopped by the bronze statue in Paddington Station, she was shocked at the outpouring of affection for her father.

People crowded around the statue and laid toys and flowers at the bear's feet. Jar after jar of marmalade had been tied with silk ribbons and left with the statue. Many people announced that they would eat a marmalade sandwich or spread marmalade on their toast the next morning to remember Michael.

Celebrities from many different countries talked about how much they'd enjoyed Michael and his books. Hugh Bonneville, the actor who played Mr. Brown in the movies, heard of Michael's passing on the last day of shooting on the second film.

"Michael created a character whose enthusiasm and optimism has given pleasure to millions," Hugh said. "Long live the bear from darkest Peru."

As a child, Michael didn't realize one day the trains he loved so much would also honor his legacy. But in 2017, it all came full circle when the Great Western Railway unveiled the Michael Bond on Platform 1 of Paddington Station.

Anyone who travels to London these days can board the train named for Michael and his beloved bear. The Great Western Railway put Michael's full name and an

Great Western Railway train named for Michael Bond/Paddington Bear. *Peter Shone/Dreamstime*

illustration on the front of a train. The last car displays Paddington's name, and the car doors have images from the films.

Even people who can't go to London can see Paddington in the night sky. The University of Birmingham's Astronomical Society named a constellation based on the beloved bear. The cub-shaped cluster of stars can be seen best in the winter season. While most bears spend months slumbering, Paddington twinkles from above.

• • • • •

Standing guard like a gatekeeper, the Paddington Bear statue watches a crowd of people leaving Platform 1. Each among them has their own plotline—the father and daughter coming back from winter holiday, the businessman on his mobile phone speaking frantically in Hindi while hailing a cab. Paddington watches two children disappear from sight as they dive into the Underground, destined for exotic places like King's Cross and Liverpool Street.

Finally, the conductor's voice crackles over a loudspeaker. He calls for all passengers to climb aboard for the next departure. They ascend the steps, jostling their way to an empty bench. From the last window seat, an elderly man tips his hat and gives Paddington a familiar wink. The bronze bear seems to nod back as though there's an unspoken secret between them.

Bibliography

BBC News. "Obituary: Michael Bond." June 28, 2017. www
.bbc.com/news.

Bond, Michael. *Bears and Forebears: A Life so Far.* HarperCollins, 1996.

BookPeople. "10 Things You Didn't Know About Michael
Bond." Accessed January 22, 2018. www.thebookpeople
.co.uk.

Burton, Sally. "End of Paddington Bear Production in
Doncaster." *Doncaster Free Press,* February 11, 2018. www
.doncasterfreepress.co.uk.

Byrne, Eleanor. "Paddington Bear Is a Symbol of Kindness to
Refugees We Should Never Forget." *Quartz,* July 2, 2017.
www.qz.com.

Cassell, Paul. "Reading Remembers the Day the Bombs Fell."
GetReading, February 14, 2013. www.getreading.co.uk
/news.

Dwyer, Colin. "Michael Bond, the 'Giant' Behind Paddington Bear, Dies at 91." *The Two-Way*, NPR, June 28, 2017.
www.npr.org/sections/thetwo-way.

Express. "Train Named After Paddington Bear Creator
Michael Bond Unveiled by His Daughter." January 10,
2018. www.express.co.uk/news.

Forsey, Zoe. "The Strange—but Very Important—Link
Between Jeremy Clarkson and Paddington Bear." *Mirror*,
June 29, 2017. www.mirror.co.uk/news.

French, Alice. "Londoners are Leaving Marmalade at the
Paddington Bear Statue to Pay Tribute to Michael Bond."
Time Out London, June 29, 2017. www.timeout.com
/london.

Gates, Anita. "Michael Bond, Paddington Bear Creator, Is
Dead at 91." *New York Times,* June 28, 2017.

Geiling, Natasha. "Why Do We Eat Popcorn at the Movies?" *Smithsonian*, October 3, 2013. www.smithsonianmag
.com/arts-culture.

Glanfield, Emma. "Queen's Birthday Celebrations Sees Kate
Middleton, Prince William and Harry Attend." *Daily Mail*,
June 10, 2016. www.dailymail.co.uk/news.

Goodman, Ernest, and Melissa Hacker. "Kindertransport:
European History." Encyclopædia Britannica, March 20,
2019. www.britannica.com/event/Kindertransport.

Great Western Railway. "New Intercity Express Train to Be
Named After Paddington Bear Author Michael Bond."
News page. January 11, 2018. www.gwr.com/about-us
/media-centre/news.

Hare, Raymond. "Foreign Affairs Oral History Project:
Ambassador Raymond A. Hare." Interview by Dayton

Mak. Association for Diplomatic Studies and Training, July 22, 1987. www.adst.org.

History. "First Paddington Bear Book is Published." This Day in History Calendar. October 13, 2016. www.history .co.uk.

Horwell, Veronica. "Michael Bond Obituary." *Guardian*, June 28, 2017.

Katz, Brigit. "Michael Bond, Creator of Paddington Bear, Dies at 91." *Smithsonian*, June 28, 2017. www.smithsonian mag.com/smart-news.

Kovalchik, Kara. "11 Things We No Longer See in Movie Theaters." *Mental Floss*, December 10, 2015. www.mental floss.com.

Lambert, Victoria. "Paddington Bear Creator Michael Bond: 'I Could have Pasted My Room with Rejection Slips. But I Never Gave Up.'" *Telegraph*, June 28, 2017.

Lang, Kirsty. "Paddington Creator Michael Bond Makes Cameo in New Film." BBC News, October 31, 2014. www .bbc.com/news.

Legacy.com. "Michael Bond Obituary." Accessed January 19, 2018. www.legacy.com/ns/michael-bond-obituary/185935631.

Listverse Staff. "11 Facts About the End of the Great War." Listverse, February 15, 2010. www.listverse.com.

Llewellyn Smith, Julia. "Michael Bond: 'I Was Worried That I'd Let Paddington Down. . . .'" *Telegraph*, November 23, 2014.

Mead, Rebecca. "Paddington Bear, Refugee." *New Yorker*, June 28, 2017.

Midgley, Emma. "Paddington Bear 'Inspired by Evacuees' Says Author Bond." BBC News, February 13, 2012. www. bbc.com/news.

Oxford University Press. "Michael Bond." Accessed January 30, 2018. www.global.oup.com/education/content/children/authors/michael-bond.

Paddington (website). "Michael Bond, the Creator of Paddington." Heritage page. Accessed January 29, 2018. www.paddington.com.

The Paddington Collective. "About Gabrielle Designs." Accessed February 2, 2018. www.thepaddingtoncollective.squarespace.com.

Palmer, Camilla. "Michael Bond: my Family Values." *Guardian*, April 1, 2016.

Preston, John. "Michael Bond Interview: 'The Modern World Is Depressing. Paddington Is My Escape.'" *Telegraph,* June 28, 2017.

Probst, Caroline. "Paddington Bear Creator Michael Bond Dies." Intellectual Takeout, June 28, 2017. www.intellectualtakeout.org.

Retter, Emily. "Michael Bond's Last Major Interview: 'Paddington Bear Is Real and I Hope He Comes With Me When I Die.'" *Mirror,* June 28, 2017. www.mirror.co.uk/news.

Reuben, Susan. "Paddington Bear: His Secret Jewish Heritage." *Jewish Chronicle,* June 29, 2017. www.thejc.com/comment/comment/.

Royal Air Force Museum. "Second World War Flying Training." *Taking Flight.* Online Exhibitions. Accessed February 2, 2018. www.rafmuseum.org.uk.

Scott, Hugh. "The Origin Story of Paddington Bear Is an Incredible Piece of History." Brainjet, July 3, 2017. www.brainjet.com.

Spencer, Julie. "Spot Paddington Bear in the Sky as Author Michael Bond Is Celebrated With Star Constellation."

GetReading, December 13, 2017. www.getreading.co.uk /whats-on.

United States Holocaust Memorial Museum. "Kindertransport, 1938-1940." Holocaust Encyclopedia. Accessed January 30, 2018. www.ushmm.org.

Verkaik, Robert. "Stop abusing child refugees (says illegal immigrant from Darkest Peru)." *Independent*, December 14, 2009. www.independent.co.uk/news.

Vincent, Alice. "Paddington Bear: 13 Things You Didn't Know." *Telegraph*, June 10, 2014.

Words for Life. "Michael Bond." Accessed February 1, 2018. www.wordsforlife.org.uk.

Zimmerman, Dwight Jon. "Operation Pied Piper: The Evacuation of English Children During World War II." Defense Media Network, December 31, 2011.

Index

Note: Page numbers in *italics* refer to photographs.